# HISTORY AND THE THEOLOGY OF LIBERATION

# HISTORY
# AND THE THEOLOGY
# OF LIBERATION

*A Latin American Perspective*

*Enrique Dussel*

*Translated by John Drury*

ORBIS BOOKS
MARYKNOLL    NEW YORK

Originally published as *Caminos de liberación latinoamericana I: Interpretación histórica de nuestro continente latinoamericano* by Latinoamerica Libros, Casilla de Correo 161, 12 (B), Buenos Aires, Argentina

Library of Congress Catalog Card Number: 75-21773

Cloth: ISBN 0-88344-1799     Paper: ISBN 0-88344-1802

Manufactured in the United States of America

# CONTENTS

Preface to the English Edition    ix

Preface to the First Spanish-Language Printing    xi

Preface to the Second Spanish-Language Printing    xv

CHAPTER 1

Theology and Liberation History    1

    *Logos* as Revelation in History    1

    Faith as Day-to-Day Interpretation of History    5

    Redefining Theology    6

    Faith and the Ordinary Charism of Prophecy    8

    Church History and Cultural History    11

    Faith as Supernatural Understanding of Existence    16

    Historicity in the Consciousness of Primitive
        Christianity    21

    Theology Is Hellenized    23

    History Is Forgotten    24

    Church History Becomes Merely Profane History    27

    Lack of Roots and Alienation    28

    Towards a Latin American Theology    29

CHAPTER 2

Major Stages of World and Church History    37

    The Origins of Man    37

    Neolithic Culture    40

v

The Indo-Europeans    54

The Semites    58

The Phenomenon of Christianity    63

Christian Persecution in the Roman Empire    67

Christendom as a System    70

Byzantine, Latin, and Hispanic Christendom    73


CHAPTER 3

Colonial Christendom in Latin America    75

The Only Colonial Version of Christendom    75

The First Prophets in Latin America    82

The First Steps (1492–1519)    85

The Evangelization of Mexico and Peru (1519–1551)    87

The Organization of the Church (1551–1620)    89

The Seventeenth Century in Hispano-America    93

The Bourbon Decadence (1700–1808)    95

The Social Struggle and the Martyr Bishops    96

Colonial Christendom in Crisis (1808–1825)    98

The Decadence Continues in a Conservative Mold
    (1825–1850)    101

Rupture Takes Place (1850–1929)    103

The Attempt to Build a "New Christendom"    106

The Worldwide Crisis of Christian Cultures    107

The Present Situation    107


CHAPTER 4

Significant Events of the Last Decade (1962–1972)    111

Vatican II (1962–1965)    111

The Medellín Conference (1968)    113

The *Coups d'état* in Brazil and Peru    116

The Church Confronts Socialism in Cuba    120

The Reality of Violence in Latin America    122

The Attitude of Bishops and Priests    128

Changing Structures and the Attitude of the Laity    131

Christian Social and Political Commitment    132

Private Property    135


CHAPTER 5

Theological Reflections on Liberation    139

The Rise of Latin American Theology    140

The Influence of Politics on Theology and
    Liberation    141

Theological Categories    145

The Dialectical Categories of Dominator and
    Dominated    145

The Dialectical Interplay of Elite and Masses    146

The Temporal Dialectic    148

Cultural Dependence and Latin American Theology    151

The Fundamental Categories    152


CHAPTER 6

Concrete Pastoral Applications    157

Critical Questioning and Openness to the
    Unexpected    157

Cultural Conditioning    159

Economic Conditioning    160

Political Conditioning    161

Religious Conditioning: Folk Catholicism    162

Liberation and "Tranquillity of Order"    164

Basic Features of a Christian Option    165

No Recipes or Prefabricated Formulas    167

Conclusion    169

Appendix: A Latin American People in the United States    171

Chronology of the Latin American Church    179

Bibliography    183

# Preface
## to the English Edition

The oil crisis in only the beginning of the end for Neolithic man. Over ten thousand years ago mankind began to exploit the land as it engaged in agriculture and the animal world as it tended its flocks. From the very beginning the exploitation of nature also included man's oppression of man: as the hunted and enslaved enemy, as the feudal serf, as the oppressed nations of colonialism and neocolonialism. The *center* (Europe, Russia, the United States, and Japan) extracted its raw materials at low cost from the countries of the *periphery* (Latin America, Black Africa, the Arab World, India and Southeast Asia, and, until recently, China).

A short time ago, *the theology of liberation* came on the scene as protest and Christian discourse. It is a challenge to the closed system, the totality represented by modern European and North American theology, that is, the theology of the center. *Liberation* occurs in history (that is, in the economic, cultural, political, sexual orders), but historical liberation is also a sign of eschatological liberation. Liberation is not disembodied "spiritualism," nor does it represent immanentistic absolutes (of those who absolutize "the world"). The theology of liberation takes on history with its eschatological sense. It is neither escapist eschatologism nor fetishistic historicism. It is the history of liberation based on a real Christ, poor among the poor—among the poor *nations*, the poor *classes, real poor people.*

The United States is confronted with an enormous responsibility, namely, that of being an imperial nation exercising worldwide domination. This status at one time may have seemed like an accomplishment of "good sense"; it now involves the contradiction of continuing to be all-powerful.

The Vietnam debacle, Watergate, the oil crisis have created a certain level of consciousness, of guilt. The theology of liberation is the protest of dominated peoples. As such it can provide a certain clarity with regard to the causes of this guilt.

> *E.D.*
> *Mendoza, Argentina*
> *1975*

# Preface
## to the First Spanish-language Printing

The six lectures in this volume were originally delivered orally as part of a longer course at the Latin American Pastoral Institute in Quito and the Liturgical Institute in Medellín.[1] In their present form they were delivered in Buenos Aires in November 1971. They followed a simple format and were set in a simple framework. That basic framework can be seen in the subtitles which have been added in this volume.

It should be kept in mind that these chapters were originally presented as spoken lectures by one Latin American to other Latin Americans. Traces of this fact are evident in this printed edition. They could not be eliminated entirely without destroying the whole thrust of their delivery. They are words *spoken* to people, not words *typed* in the privacy of a comfortable study. They are spoken discourse, not textbook material.

The lectures present and discuss the following theses. Against the broad backdrop of various neolithic cultures, of various Semitic cultures in particular, the apostolic community in Palestine was transformed into a Church that was scattered and persecuted throughout the Mediterranean basin. Marginal elements of it also took root outside the Roman empire. From the fourth century A.D. on, it constituted what we here call Christendom [*Cristiandad*]: that is, a religious and cultural system with political, economic, and various other facets. In this system, the existential experience of the Christian was linked with hellenistic ways of conceptualizing existence. What concerns us here is Latin Christendom in the West, specifically the Spanish version of it that came to America bearing traces of the modern Europe that was then taking shape. The hispanic or Latin American Church is the product of a vast and lengthy process which mirrored what was taking place on the European continent at various stages. Colonial domination, the secularization of life, and the crisis of European modernization have ushered in a new and unforeseen state of affairs.

There is another important point to be kept in mind. If a person wishes to engage in theological reflection in Latin America, he must first know and appreciate the conditions which allow for the very possibility of reflection or thinking. If this thinking is to be Christian as well, it must take into account the fact of cultural dependence and the fact that the cultural system known as Christendom is disintegrating. That is the situation which confronts the thinker, the historian, the philosopher, and the theologian in Latin America. They all must take note of, and try to provide solutions for, the new situation that is arising as we move beyond Christendom, the modernist outlook, and the imperial "will to power."

This presupposes a whole new horizon of understanding, a whole hermeneutic structure which is not yet accessible to the average Christian or even to the theologian himself in some instances. In practice it calls for a new existential outlook that will formulate the issues in a way which will measure up to the urgent demands imposed on us by the whole question of Latin American liberation. It is a disturbing and risky situation because it is essentially a prophetic situation. Our position will be denigrated and criticized by unfounded progressivism and by integralist traditionalism. But the way to a Christian solution to the present-day crisis in Latin America is clear. As Jesus said to his disciples: "Follow me, and let the dead bury their dead" (Matt. 8:22).

From this historical city, where the Latin American Church had something akin to a new Pentecost,

*E.D.*

*Medellín, Colombia*
*1972*

## NOTES

1. For further study of the topics treated in these chapters, the reader may consult the following works by the same author: "América latina y conciencia cristiana," *Cuadernos IPLA,* no. 8, Quito, 1970 (French version in *Espirit,* 7–8, 1965, pp. 2–20); "Iberoamérica en la historia universal," *Revista de Occidente,* 1965, 25:85–95; "Cultura, cultura latinoamericana y cultura nacional," *Cuyo* (UNC Mendoza), 4 (1968), pp. 4–40; *Historia de la Iglesia en América Latina* (Barcelona: Nova Terra, 1974); *El humanismo semita* (Buenos Aires: Eudeba, 1969); "From Secularization to Secularism: Science from the Renaissance to the Enlightenment," in *Concilium,* no. 47 (New York: Paulist, 1969), pp. 93–119; *Para una historia del catolicismo popular en Argentina* (Buenos Aires: Cuadernos Bonum, 1970); *Les évêques latinoaméricains, défenseurs de l'indien (1504–1620)* (Wiesbaden: Steiner, 1970); *Para una de-strucción de la historia de la ética* (Paraná: Universidad del Litoral, 1971); *Para una ética de la liberación latinoamericana,* 3 vols. (Buenos Aires; Siglo XXI, 1973); *Método para una filosofía de la liberación* (Salamanca: Sígueme, 1974), "Domination-Liberation," in *Concilium,* no. 96 (New York: Herder, 1974), pp. 34–56.

# Preface
## to the Second Spanish-language Printing

The first printing of this unpretentious little book was sold out in a few months. This suggests that there is a growing interest in everything that is distinctively our own—not only in the topics treated but also in the methodology employed. Since I delivered a second series of lectures in 1972, this volume has now become the first volume in a series. The second volume, *Ethics and the Theology of Liberation,* is to appear in the near future. It will probe more deeply into topics that were merely alluded to in this present volume. In the years to come I hope to continue this annual lecture series and to shed greater light on the critical questions that now face Latin American Christians who seek to involve themselves in a committed way with the poor and with the whole process of liberation.

The criticism directed against our Latin American theology, which my friend Gustavo Gutiérrez was the first to call the "theology of liberation," suggests that there is something solid to it after all. Some months ago a group of Christian thinkers from Latin America gathered at the tomb of Philip II in El Escorial. (Our statements and conclusions have been published by the house of Sígueme in Salamanca: *Fe cristiana y cambio social an América Latina,* 1973.) There our views were heard by people from the very nations that had conquered us a few centuries ago. They listened to us attentively and even admiringly. This positive attitude suggests that Europe is beginning to glimpse in our Christian reflection—poor in material resources but rich in reality—a new phase in world theology.

This short book is a sketchy historical contribution to that theology. Volume 2 will provide a more systematic reflection on the theology of praxis, the theology of politics, and theological epistemology.

The whole job remains to be done, not because nothing has been done but because each generation must do the whole job over again, particularly when the situation is as critical as that of Latin America. Each generation must start from its novel situation; it must use its liberty created in order to effect and live out a *new moment* in the one and only history there is: the history of messianic liberation, the history of salvation. Traditionalism imitates and astutely tries to reconcile the irreconcilable; tradition lives the newness of creation, the unending re-creation effected by our Liberator, who is Other than any sort of closed, prefabricated totality. This is a discontinuous, critical moment which keeps pushing human beings forward when they try to wallow in their achievements of injustice and oppression.

Here in the Cathedral of Lima, near the tomb of Toribio de Mogrovejo and not far from the tomb of the half-breed Martin de Porres, who was not allowed into the Dominican choir, I express my belief in the liberation of Latin America. And I look forward to it hopefully as a sign of our eschatological liberation.

*E.D.*
*Lima, Peru*
*1973*

# 1

# Theology and Liberation History

We shall try to interpret the crisis in which we now find ourselves as a Church and a culture, both in the world at large and here in Latin America itself. The crisis is so thoroughgoing that we must start with the very beginnings of mankind. Only then will we be able to appreciate its depth and to understand why it has so upset everyone living in our era—particularly Latin American Christians.

## *LOGOS* AS REVELATION IN HISTORY

We talk about theo-logy and the theo-logian. We are thereby referring to a *logos* about God (Greek *theos*). Here *logos* refers to "comprehension" or "understanding"; it is a task of gathering together, taking in, embracing. When I comprehend something, I take it in and embrace it. But if that is the case, then it would seem to be impossible for us to comprehend God. How are finite, human creatures to embrace, to comprehend, the unembraceable Infinite?

So we confront our first problem. Is it *possible* to have any *logos* about God? And if the answer to that question is yes, then under what conditions is such a *logos* possible? It is possible only on the condition that God re-veals or un-veils himself. He must strip away the veil which hides himself from us and make himself comprehensible to the finite. He,

1

the Infinite, will be comprehensible to us by virtue of his revelation and the way in which he choses to grant it to us.

As we know very well, this revelation is historical—and *only* historical—in nature. The only locus of revelation is history. The only *locus theologicus* is history, the concrete history we live each day. If we do not discover the *sense and import* of history, we will not be able to comprehend God's revelation to us either. God—the Infinite, the Other—reveals himself to man in history. This simple statement, so summarily presented, is the whole essence of theology. It is the whole essence of the historical process as a history of liberation and a "pasch" of justice and liberation.

Let us begin our reflection here with a biblical text—specifically, with the third chapter of the book of Exodus. Moses is in the desert. He has not gone there to do penance or to acquire perfection. He has fled to the desert because he has killed an Egyptian. In some way he had "discovered" the lowly Hebrew and taken a stand on his behalf, killing an Egyptian in the process. He flees from his potential persecutors and heads for the desert.

In the desert silence reigns. In such silence one begins to learn how to "hear" the Other. The desert is a vast expanse where our own words gradually are stilled. We become all ears; we are able to hear the words of the Other. Thus the desert is not an "ascesis," a process of ascending the ladder of perfection. It is rather an opening up, an expectant waiting. The person in the desert waits hopefully for the mystery that might reveal itself. To sojourn in the desert is to listen for something, to learn how to listen well. It is not a dialectic between imperfection and perfection, between impurity and purity; it is a dialectic between spoken word and hearing.

So Moses is in the desert. He is in a structured totality of meaning, the totality of the desert. There he is living comfortably as a herdsman with his wife, his father-in-law, and his flocks. Of course he is not yet the prophet that he will be later on. He is a herdsman, comfortably established in his day-to-day routine and perfectly adapted to his world. Then one day, we are told, he "looked" and "saw" a "fire flaming out of a bush." It was an object of his *vision*. He saw only the flame at first; he did not see the word that summoned him from the midst of the bush. Then he heard a word which he did not see. "Word" in the Hebrew language is *dabar*; in Greek it is translated as *logos*. But the Hebrew word does not denote "comprehension," as the Greek word does; rather, it denotes "revelation," as it does in John's Gospel. It is a creating, pro-creating, innovating word. This "word" calls the herdsman by name: "Moses! Moses!" First Moses saw something—the flame; then he heard someone pro-voking him, calling him forth, beyond what he saw before him.

Moses *heard* a voice. It *said* something to him. This is a basic point for us because of the situation in which we find ourselves. Comfortably established in another totality, not the totality of the desert but the totality of daily life and its hubbub, we do not hear anything. We, like Moses, are being called by name continually; but we do not hear anyone or anything. In Hebrew there is an idiom which deals with this phenomenon. A person's hearing or ears are said to be

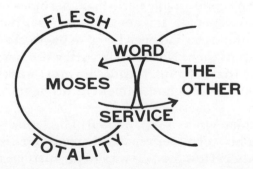

"closed" or "open." We read in the Bible that Solomon was a "wise" man, a man who possessed "wisdom." That is the Greek version of the Hebrew text. The Hebrew text says that Solomon had an "open ear." In other words, he knew how to listen.

Moses, then, heard words being spoken to him. What did they say? "I have witnessed . . . have heard." Note the dialogical movement here. God, the Other, has also seen and heard. He has heard the people's "cry of complaint." It, too, is a word. But it is more like a lament because it reveals the sorrow of an enslaved people. God says: "I . . . have heard their cry of complaint against their slave drivers." God is revealing himself to Moses now because he has heard his people's cry. Moses, in turn, hears what God says: "Liberate my people . . . out of Egypt."

Moses, the herdsman comfortably ensconced in the desert, is suddenly confronted with a message which he, in his egotism, would have preferred not to have heard at all. In this respect he is much like Jonah, who tried to flee when he heard that he was supposed to go to Nineveh and preach repentance. He ran away, but a large fish swallowed him up. Jonah is not a real figure in history; he is a fictional character. But his story points up the fact that the prophetic calling is a tremendous responsibility rather than an honorary privilege.

Moses, the comfortable herdsman, becomes the liberator of an enslaved people. It is not an honor but a harsh responsibility insofar as he had been living in the totality of his own egotism up to then. Now he will suffer the persecution of the totality that is Egypt, because he must somehow shoulder the injustice and enslavement of his people in order to free them.

Our human vision is very limited. The Other who reveals himself in his word ever remains beyond our vision insofar as he is Other. How then do we situate ourselves before the Other as Other? We do so through faith.

## FAITH AS DAY-TO-DAY
## INTERPRETATION OF HISTORY

Faith is an act of understanding, a way of seeing. But faith knows that it remains with something which it cannot transcend; it remains there, knowing that there is something more. But who or what is it that goes beyond what is seen? First of all, *hope*—the hope that the Other will reveal himself. In the concrete, this comes down to *love* for the Other as Other. It is love that goes beyond the surface vision, the flaming bush which is the sign of the Other's presence. Every day we look at the surface of a person, at his or her face. But the face does not open us up to that person as the incomprehensible mystery of liberty that he or she is. We look at individuals and groups around us every day. We see them, but we do not see them as a free and mysterious Other.

We must acknowledge that our vision stops at the surface. We must wait hopefully for the revelation of the Other as Other in and through love. Only then can the Other reveal to us what lies hidden in the novel mystery of his liberty. Faith, hope, and charity are concrete anthropological attitudes for our day-to-day life in the real world. The love in question here is not some vague, general sort of love. It is a *love for justice* because it is a love for the Other as Other. It is a love for what is "Other" in him. It is a love for the Other insofar as the Other is not me; insofar as the Other has his own rights; insofar as the Other pro-vokes me and calls me forth, calling my attention to his rights and demanding just treatment from me. That is how God reveals himself to Moses. He approaches the comfortable pastor in the desert and bids him to free the chosen people of God.

This dialogical structure will enable us to understand and appreciate what theology is. Having described the conditions which make listening possible, we must now consider the meaning of the revelatory word. What does it say? It does not just tell us what God as Other is; it also tells us what is happening in the concrete as far as God is concerned. God sees what is happening to us and *reveals* its meaning to us. He reveals himself to us in and by revealing the "sense" or "meaning" of day-to-day history.

A whole people was enslaved in Egypt. Moses, living in the desert, had not comprehended this people as such: i.e., as slaves in Egypt. Once God reveals to him that they are enslaved, Moses includes the world of these slaves in his own world and thereby discovers the meaningful connection between their slavery and his own life. To put it another way: I do not see God, but by faith he reveals to me the meaning of what I do see. And what is seen by me are historical events. Once they had no meaning for me. Thanks to divine revelation, however, they enter into my world with new meaningfulness.

That is what happened to Moses. The once carefree herdsman is suddenly plagued by pangs of conscience. If he does not go out and liberate his people, he will be conscious of having committed sin. If he remains in the desert, he will be a traitor to the call he has received. Faith does not permit me to see what is revealed to me. Rather, it enables me to see the import and meaning of happenings in history where the word of God is at work and where I will carry out my role as a Christian.

## REDEFINING THEOLOGY

So "theology" means thinking about God, about a God who reveals himself in history. To believe God's revelation is to comprehend and embrace the import of what he reveals to us. In other words, it is to comprehend and embrace the meaning of history. There is nothing paradoxical about Jesus' statement that good done to the poor is good done to him. It is a simple truth. The person who sees a free Other in the poor and liberates the slave from Egypt is the person who truly loves God, for the slave in Egypt is the very epiphany of God himself. If a person opens up to the slave in Egypt, he opens up to God; if he shuts out the slave in Egypt, he shuts out God. The person who does not commit himself to the liberation of the slaves in Egypt is an atheist. He is Cain killing Abel. Once Abel was dead, Cain was alone. He now believed himself to be the only One, the Eternal. He presented himself as a pantheistic god. That was the temptation posed to Adam in the garden: "You will be like gods." To be like God is to pretend to be the one and only being; to refuse to open up to the Other, who has been murdered.

God, however, keeps on revealing himself to us as the Other who summons us. He is the first Other. If I do not listen to my fellow man in bondage, then I am not listening to God either. If I do not commit myself to the liberation of my fellow man, then I am an atheist. Not only do I not love God, I am actually fighting against God because I am affirming my own divinity.

Theology, then, is a *logos* which ponders God revealing himself in history.

What about *pastoral theology*? "Pastoral" comes from the word "pastor," which means shepherd. However, it does not refer to the shepherd or herdsman nicely established in the desert with his family and flock. It refers to the poor and lowly shepherd who must confront the pharaoh in order to free his people, without even knowing exactly what to say or how to say it. Once this goal is achieved, it is the pastor who must pass over and through the desert. This passover (*pesah* in Hebrew) occurs in a second desert. It is not the desert of the comfortably settled shepherd. It is the desert through which Moses guides his people in the process of liberation. Once again it is a process of historical discernment. Which way do we go? What is the meaning and purpose of the whole process? Only the person who has faith can find out, for only such a person knows how to open up to God's revelatory word and to discover its concrete import.

Hence pastoral theology is a way of pondering the journey of God's people as they seek liberation in the desert. And this journey towards liberation is a *passover,* a passover from bondage to total liberation. The Hebrew word alludes to the ongoing paschal resurrection. Pastoral activity is paschal; it is our passage through the desert that leads to liberation.

Passolini has a curious film entitled *Teorema.* He uses an unexpected motif—sexuality—to deal with the same theme we are discussing here. At the heart of this film is a human being, naked at the end, who is running through the desert towards God. That is precisely the thesis of Kierkegaard: We are naked creatures in the desert, running towards God; we are poor, wretched creatures without anything, who must open up to God. In a sense, we are dealing with the passage of humanity through the desert of liberation history.

## FAITH AND THE ORDINARY
## CHARISM OF PROPHECY

If we are to be pastors and if theology is to enlighten us, we must be able to discover the sense and meaning of the historical present. Discovering the meaning of the present—note that I say the present, not the future—is called *prophecy.* Here I am not talking about prophecy as an extraordinary charism. I am talking about it as the thing that goes to make up the day-to-day life of real Christian faith. Jesus said that we would be able to move mountains if we had faith as small as the mustard seed. Well, the mountains with which I am familiar are pretty quiet; so our faith must be very small indeed. Prophecy is part of this faith held by the Christian people.

The word "prophecy" comes from a Greek word (*profēmi*) which means "to speak out before someone." The prophet speaks out before the people, telling them the meaning of the events that are taking place here and now. Moses stands before the enslaved Israelites and tells them that Yahweh has sent him to liberate them. He stands before the pharaoh and tells him to let the Israelites go. The Hebrew text then tells us that the pharaoh "hardened his heart." For the Hebrews, the heart was the seat of man's liberty. The Bible is telling us that the pharaoh lost his freedom because he had sinned, because he was exercising domination over other human beings.

Then Moses asked God for the gift of liberation, and the plagues began. How would we describe those plagues today in sociological terms? If the water supply of some large city was turned to blood today, would it not smack of sabotage? Then came the other plagues, culminating in the horrendous death of all the firstborn in Egypt. Only this last terror changed the mind of the unjust oppressor. He let the Israelites go, not out of a sense of justice but out of fear. Pharaoh changed his mind again and sent his army out in pursuit of the Israelites. His army was swallowed up in the Red Sea.

How much violence there is in this whole story! And we must give this violence consideration too, because all these questions must be examined in any Latin American theology.

Moses is a prophet because he spells out the meaning of events before the people. The point he makes is that they have been enslaved and that now God chooses to liberate them. Here pastoral theology becomes reflection on the praxis of liberation. Christian praxis must be committed to the day-to-day liberation process of people; it must seek to discover the ultimate eschatological meaning of that process.

Let me give an example of what I mean by this. When I open the morning paper, I should know how salvation history is working itself out through everything that is happening. I should not say: "I don't understand anything that is going on in this country or around the world." The person who feels "lost" in the face of events—be they political, economic, cultural, religious, or spiritual—is a person who has little or no faith. He must ask for an increase of faith, because he does not discern the import and meaning of the present. In such a case this individual leaves home in the morning and heads for work. He may want to serve his fellow men. But he does not know how to do it, and his work may actually be a disservice that directly contradicts the message of the Gospel. Since he does not know where the meaning of events lies, he may perform many meaningless things.

This is an important point. There is no sense in trying to shore up a building or reinforce it if we have not asked ourselves whether the building is worth saving in the first place. Perhaps we have not noticed that other people are at work laying the foundations of another building, that there is where we should be too. It is most important for us to discover the sense and meaning of things, because all our activity will depend on that. We can waste a whole lifetime in useless labor. As the old saying goes: The road to hell is paved with good intentions. But it is not just our intention that can go astray; our whole effort can be misguided. We must work for something that God really wants. We must use all our intelligence and will to get closer to what God wants to reveal to us in the difficult but adventurous times in which we live. What is taking place before our eyes is wondrous, even though we may not notice it at times. I think we are at the dawn of a great phase of Church history, and this applies in particular to the Church in Latin America. That is what I shall try to bring out in the remarks which follow.

But before I pursue that topic further, I would like to clarify a few points for those of you who have some acquaintance with theology. I should like to indicate how Church history came to be separated from dogmatic theology; how theology lost its roots in history so that we now find it difficult to comprehend the day-to-day reality around us. We must rediscover a great brand of theology that we have forgotten. Right now I should like to sketch how all this happened, and I want to begin with our own history as an example.

## CHURCH HISTORY AND CULTURAL HISTORY

The difficulty we face in trying to expound a history of the Church in Latin America derives from the fact that there is no written history of Latin American culture. In his book, *América en la historia* ("America in History"), Leopoldo Zea notes that we are constantly trying to find out what is native to America; but in the process we discover that "America is outside history."

If we examine the great expositions of the history of world culture, we find that Latin America is not given adequate consideration. In one such history of culture, for example, Alfred Weber devotes only a few remarks to Latin America. He notes that Portugal and Spain prompted a European expansion which resulted in the conquest of America. That is the sum total of his treatment of Latin America.

Latin America receives this treatment, in general, because the great cultural historians are Europeans or North Americans, not Latin Americans. We have no one of world stature. But that is not the only reason. The fact is that we ourselves are ignorant of our history. Latin America remains on the outskirts of history. To have a Church history, we must have a cultural history. So far we lack that cultural history. If we are to find our place as Christians in Latin America, we must first find our place as Latin Americans in the history of world culture.

Because we are "outside history," we have necessarily fallen prey to an inauthentic historicity. Here a few words of explanation are in order.

As we know, contemporary existentialist thought talks about temporality—i.e., the time dimension. The being of man is not like the being of things. It is not merely a present; it is a has-been which now is in the process of being by virtue of its potentiality to be. The being of man can be comprehended only in the time dimension, in the framework of temporality. It can be comprehended only in terms of its three phases or instances: that is, as a has-been, which is now in the process of being, by virtue of its potentiality to be. The "potentiality to be" is the future. In German the word for future is *Zu-kunft,* that which is "coming to" or "approaching." This suggests the paradoxical nature of the future. The future is something towards which we are going but which is also coming towards us. Thus the future is not "what I shall do." It is the actual and operative presence of what I understand as my potentiality to be. It constitutes the fundamental instance of what today is called "temporality."

Temporality, in turn, is merely the bedrock of one of its modes which we refer to as "historicity." Historicity is not simply temporality. It is the way, the mode, in which mankind lives its temporality in the concrete—and at all times. Man is *in* history only because the human realm and man himself is *already* historical. It is man who "historifies" what he lives "within" the world. A historical document, for example, is not historical in and of itself. It is historical because it was in and of man's hand. It is historical because it was in man's world, not because it is now in the world. It is historical because it *was* in the human world.

Historicity can be lived in various ways. We as Latin Americans are "outside history." This inevitably means that we are dragged down into an inauthentic brand of historicity. In our case inauthentic historicity means "historify-ing" the things at hand (i.e., turning them into history) and interpreting them in a superficial, commonplace fashion which really covers them up and conceals them. The result is that our authentic tradition remains in the dark.

We must not equate "traditionalism" with authentic tradition. Traditionalism stops at ontic comprehension, and "ontic" is on the same level as "superficial" and "commonplace." These terms suggest that tradition does indeed transmit something, but in this transmission it conceals more than it reveals to us. It transmits to us only what is *superficial and obvious.* For example, it is obvious that we are Latin Americans. But the real point is to know what that really means. The more we dwell on the surface of what we are, the more our real inner nature and life remains concealed from us. Tradition transmits everything to us—language, for example. Now at first glance it might seem that language is an indifferent reality which poses no problems at all. We fail to take cognizance of the fact that language is not only a tool for communication, but also a trap. It is a trap because the very words of a language conceal the experience of a people; they cover over that experience. We do not realize that when a given people does not possess a certain set of experiences, it has no word for those experiences. When an attempt is made to transmit a certain experience from one people to another, which may or may not have words for the experience, it is quite possible that translation will be impossible and that the experience may therefore be ignored or forgotten.

Authentic historicity is critical, dialectical. To be critical means to be able to "de-present" the present; to take what is commonplace and habitual and look at it in another light. It means that we can really test and probe what tradition transmits to us. One of the privileged ways of testing and checking what is handed down by tradition is history. It is one valuable way of being able to test and criticize ourselves in order to uncover what lies concealed in the obvious data.

But if we stand "outside history," then we cannot possibly use this means of engaging in criticism.

If a German college student wants to know what it means to be German, he can pick up a treatment of cultural history such as that written by Alfred Weber. If an English college student wants to do the same thing, he can read Toynbee's *Study of History.* But we Latin Americans have no equivalent interpretations of our own place in world history to which we can turn.

Let us suppose we read the books just mentioned, taking the work of Weber for our example here. Weber begins with the origins of *homo sapiens.* Then he covers prehistory, the great cultures of Antiquity, and subsequent developments. Gradually his focus narrows to Germany, so that a German can get some idea of his people's place in world history from Weber's treatment. But as we Latin Americans read the book, we find ourselves being estranged from our own history as we move towards modern times. Instead of finding a detailed discussion of the conquest of America when we get to the sixteenth century, we are treated to a detailed discussion of Martin Luther. I am not suggesting that there should not be any discussion of that great Reformation figure. But I am saying that this topic was not the fundamental problem facing *us* in the sixteenth century. Gradually Weber's narrative moves into channels that simply are not ours as Latin Americans. By the time we finish his book, we are alienated human beings—Europeanized Latin Americans.

This is happening to us every day. If we do nothing but study a history that is not our own, we end up by being something *other than what we ourselves really are.* We must ask ourselves: What is it to be Latin Americans? We really do not know because no one has taught us.

The same thing applies to Church history. Professor Joseph Lortz, my teacher in Mainz, has written a great history of the Church. He is German, as Weber is, and his

THEOLOGY AND LIBERATION HISTORY

work is a prime example of my point. Reading his great work, one might be inclined to think it really is a history of the "universal" Church. In fact, however, it is only a history of the European Church, of the Church in German-speaking areas and Central Europe. When Lortz gets to the era of the Reformation, he talks about Luther. (He is an expert on Luther.) Then he goes on to talk about the Enlightenment, Gallicanism, Ultramontanism, and so forth. He says nothing about Latin America. Thus the superficial, commonplace view within which we live our lives cannot be criticized because we study only about Europe. Our own cultural and ecclesial world lies buried under ignorance, indifference, and neglect.

Perhaps there is only one way open to us if we want to undertake critical thinking and engage in authentic historicity, if we want to "historify" what we have at hand and turn it into real history. Perhaps we must start over and try to work up a historical self-awareness that will redefine us in genetic terms.

Such an effort would certainly be "destructive" in many respects, authentically "destructive" in terms of the root meaning of the Latin word from which it comes: *de-struo*. We would really be engaged in a work of "un-building" and "dismantling." We would be taking a critical look at things which confront us as a coordinated, unified whole. We would be taking them apart to see what might lie hidden behind them.

History and the study of history is not destructive in the everyday sense of the term. It is destructive in the sense that it is a probing and a catharsis. It is, in a sense, a collective psychoanalysis of our culture. When we want to know about the traumas we carry inside ourselves, we turn to autobiography and biography; we turn to the history of ourselves. Well, history is a collective psychoanalysis in which we examine our cultural traumas and our failures at adaptation. If we want to understand the crisis of Latin American Catholicism today, we may have to look back to the sixteenth century—or perhaps even to the fourth century. We do not really know for sure where to look. Or perhaps it would be better to say that we have forgotten where to look. We are somewhat similar to a child who got a traumatic clout from his father in the distant past. The blow itself is forgotten, but its impact remains present in his psyche. Perhaps our culture experienced an analogous trauma way back in the fourth century and is only now freeing itself from the effects; hence the frightful crisis we are now experiencing.

I am not trying to espouse or justify psychoanalysis here. My point is that the example may help us to see what history can do. History can help us to "see" the process at work; and the very act of seeing what has been going on is a major part of the cure. We see the real situation that we are in and we now know why we are in it.

## FAITH AS SUPERNATURAL UNDERSTANDING OF EXISTENCE

What does it really mean to be a Christian in Latin America? First of all, we have to define in real-life terms what it means to be a Christian today in the twentieth century. Once we tackle the complex reality of Latin America, the whole question becomes even more complex. On the one hand, it seems clear that it is in the light of faith that we live out our existence here in Latin America. By the same token, however, we must re-define and re-conceptualize. That is one of the tasks that faces Catholic thinking today. It must probe the implications of historical interpretation of the faith.

I just said "re-conceptualize." Conceptualization is the process of passing from a *de facto* experience to an abstract, analytical expression of it. This process cannot help but be ambiguous at times. We must be very careful about the way we conceptualize something, about the "how" of the process. Now traditional Christian theology, and of course Western philosophy, took its inspiration from hellenic thought. This mode of thinking seemed to be merely methodological and hermeneutical. In fact, however, a specific experience of life and a specific understanding of being was woven into that way of thinking. Conceptualization can indeed shed light on certain aspects of everyday life. In the absence of *de facto* experience, however, it may leave other aspects in the dark. Such was the case in the present instance. The process of conceptualization began to give special emphasis to certain Christian experiences to which it could give expression. Other Christian experiences, for which Greek philosophic thought could not find any expression, were not conceptualized in an adequate way. The Christian faith was conceptualized only partially.

Today faith is described by some theologians as a "supernatural existential," although they do not always mean what I mean by the term here. People familiar with contemporary philosophy appreciate the import and thrust of this term as an attempt to describe the essential nature of our faith. It enables us to work out a more exact understanding of faith. Human beings have an understanding of what things are that is existential, matter-of-fact, ontic; it is called *Verstehen* in German. But faith is some kind of *new* existential understanding, as it were. Living in the "world," I have a pre-conceptual understanding of being. Faith is a *new* "world" in a sense. Thus we can take everything that is described and discussed in phenomenology and the existential thought of people like Heidegger and Jaspers, and then turn it into a completely new treatment of faith.

The term *"new* world" does not refer to a theoretical viewpoint or perspective. Faith is not a *habitus* of the theoretical mind or intellect. Faith is something that opens me to a whole new horizon of existential understanding; and it presupposes the whole of man in his pre-Christian world. "To be a Christian in Latin America" is to under-stand Latin American existence under a *new* light. But if we want to analyze this experience theologically, if we want to be able to express it to students and the people, then we must carry out a whole hermeneutical task that still remains to be done. We must attain a *new* understanding or com-prehension of existence. And this new understanding must be *dialectical*, in the sense that the original Greek word *dia-logos* suggests "moving from one horizon of com-prehension to another horizon of comprehension." As a form of understanding or comprehension, faith can never get to its last and ultimate horizon because that horizon is historical. When I think I have reached the point of under-standing everything around me with full and complete clarity, time has passed and God has already revealed him-self to man in another, more mature way. Faith, like under-standing, is dialectical and hence historical.

But what do we do? If we want to train people, we send them to Europe. There they study liturgy, catechetics, theology, and a host of other subjects. When they come back, they are completely lost in Latin America. They are out of touch and never get their feet back on the ground. They are Frenchified, Germanized, Italianized, or other-wise alienated. It is not simply a matter of reading the Gospel message. We must read it *within tradition*. And tradi-tion has come down to us, not through Italy or Germany, but through a Spain that came to America and through a concrete Church in Latin America to which we belong.

The fact is, however, that theology at some point came to lose its rootedness in history, its primary theological experi-ence. The Hebrew way of thinking in the Old Testament and Christian thinking in the New Testament were almost exclusively history-minded or "historical" in nature. Note that this was real "thinking" because it is precisely a *logos* about God we find in the Bible. We are used to hearing and imagining that the apostles were uneducated, unlettered

fishermen who did not know a great deal. We feel that
Jesus' message was for simple people and hence had no
developed methodology to it. We feel that way because we
have come to equate the methodology of Greek thought
with theological thinking as a scholarly discipline or science.
What has happened is that we have lost sight of a different
but perfectly sound and coherent logic—the logic used by
the prophets and by Jesus in his preaching. Their
methodology is a strictly theological one. It is a process of
thinking which is experientially aware of its course, but
which had not spelled out its methodology as Greek logic
did.

I cannot explain the methodology of Hebrew thinking in
a few brief words here.[1] What is clear is that it is not the
same as that of the Greek *organon*. But it is a coherent and
organized way of thinking even though it differs from that
of Aristotle. This "Hebrew theology" always contemplated
history. The Hebrews thought something like this: "What is
happening to us today is akin to what God did with Moses
and our people in the desert of Sinai." In other words, the
Hebrews found the meaning and import of the present
moment in the past history of their people. When the people of the nation arc being sent off into exile, prophets like
Isaiah and Jeremiah tell them that their imprisonment and
exile are due to their sinful actions. The meaning of what is
happening to them is to be found in history, always in
history.

From the days of ancient Israel on, historical self-
awareness comes to exist as a reality in the world. In the eyes
of the Old Testament prophets, the history of Israel is the
revelation of Yahweh. In and through this concrete history,
the nation progresses in its self-awareness. The Jew in exile
in Babylon around 550 B.C. was reflectively aware of his
nation's past, a past that began with Abraham. For him
Abraham was not a mythical figure but a concrete being in
actual history. And after him came Isaac, Jacob, and all the

other great forefathers of Israel. The book of Chronicles, for example, offers a theological interpretation of Israel's past history. Past events are recalled in order to discover some *meaning* in them. Thus the Babylonian exile is interpreted as a punishment inflicted on the Israelites by God, through an alien nation, for their sinfulness.

In short, ancient Israel continually strove to give some meaning to its past history. On the basis of this past and its meaning, Israel also tried to explain the present and glimpse the import of the future, and this is again prophecy. Israel was fully aware that its concrete existence here and now, its present safety and salvation was determined by its link to the past history of its patriarchs and forefathers.

Such was not the case with Plato and Aristotle. The Greeks did have people like Herodotus and Thucydides. They recounted things that happened in history, but they stayed on the anecdotal level. We are told, for example, that ten thousand warriors trekked so far, were defeated in battle, and then marched home again. But the doings of those ten thousand soldiers do not constitute, for someone like Aristotle, an ontological level which is adequate for defining man. Mankind is not seen to be dependent on historical happenings. Instead man is seen to be dependent on mythical happenings; i.e., the fall of a soul into a body. Because this soul is divine and therefore transhistorical, nothing that happens in time is part of its essential constitution. The Greeks were never able to get beyond anecdotal history because certain events recalled by them would inevitably be repeated again in the endless cycle of eternal return. These events did not have anything definitive in their nature. Nothing happened "once and for all."

In the writings of Saint Paul, by contrast, the notion of "once and for all" (Greek *hapax*) is very prominent. He applies it to the historical reality of Christ, and it is a central notion in his whole theology. In his book entitled *Christ and*

*Time,* Oscar Cullmann gives a clear exposition of the notion.[2] But the notion of *hapax* does not appear on the scene only with the coming of the Word. For the Jews, Abraham himself had been a *hapax* too in some sense; and so was every event from day to day.

This is so because "once and for all time" there existed this concrete human being to whom a promise was made. By associating oneself with him, one became a member of the covenant and an object of the promise; one could be saved. History becomes the constitutive element on the metaphysical level, because one cannot obtain salvation if he is not associated with Abraham and the covenant. Such could not be the case with the Greeks. It is among the Hebrews that the notion of sacred history or salvation history takes root and develops. The Psalms reiterate the theme endlessly: Our forefathers were released from Egypt and went through such and such experiences, all of which proves God's providence and his love for us. Interpreting history in their own age, the prophets propose revolutionary reforms. For the people of Israel, in short, history is a sacred history, a reflection on the past in which here and now existence takes on meaning.

## HISTORICITY IN THE CONSCIOUSNESS OF PRIMITIVE CHRISTIANITY

Now that is precisely what the New Testament proposes to us. The most clearcut example is Luke, who wrote a Gospel and the Acts of the Apostles. He describes a real-life history. The life of Jesus begins in Bethlehem, continues in Nazareth and other parts of the nation, and culminates in Jerusalem. The book of Acts picks up the subsequent life of his Church. From Jerusalem it spreads to Samaria and Antioch. Through the missionary work of Saint Paul, it eventually reaches Rome. Luke's narrative depicts the historical growth of Christianity as a widening expanse of concentric circles, which start in Bethlehem and eventually end up in Rome. Rome is seen as the center of world history and the culmination of the process.

Here Christianity begins to take cognizance of its temporality, to interpret its own evolution and growth, thereby providing itself with a theology of history. The book of Revelation, like the works of Luke, tries to engage in historical self-interpretation also. In a prophetic vein it attempts to interpret very real events that were happening to Christians in the first century A.D. It interprets the persecutions suffered by the faithful along the line of Hebrew apocalyptic theology, which is another way of theologizing in terms of the concrete, sacred happenings that are befalling a community. The whole process of objectification within the Jewish communities of the Old Testament and the early Christian communities of the New Testament is a process of historical hermeneutics. Jesus is a real, concrete child who grows in wisdom, age, and grace; and after him, the Church grows in like manner. These primeval events are described, not in anecdotal terms, but in a way *that gives them meaning and sense.* The "description" is actually a theology of history.

This process continues in the movement known as Judaeo-Christianity, which begins around 60 A.D. and continues to 100 or 120 A.D. It is noteworthy because it is a Christian movement, but a Christian movement with a Jewish apocalyptic theology. The logical instrumentation for giving expression to its experience continues to be that of Hebrew thinking; hence it continues to operate on an historical level. Revelations are offered to the community which help it to interpret the course of certain Christian phenomena. Theology is still the description of a sacred history, of liberation.

At the end of the first century after Christ, however, there is a break. Theology, which had been the description or explicitation of God's revelation in history, begins to be hellenized. There is a shift from reflective consideration of the history of God's revelation to his people to a systematic theology which presents its argument in the manner of the Greeks.

## THEOLOGY IS HELLENIZED

Clement of Alexandria, with his theory of *gnosis*, is a perfect example of the new approach. But even before him we have the early apologists, who bear clear witness to the gradual transition. They do not neglect history completely. Justin, for example, takes the history of the chosen people into account. He, like other writers, used the argument from antiquity—trying to show that the Jews were more ancient than Homer and the early Greek sages because they originated with Abraham.

Here we can see continuity in Christian consciousness. The Christian feels a sense of fellowship with Abraham, not with Homer. At the same time, however, Christians begin to accept the instruments of Greek logic and to argue in syllogisms. They still say what the prophets had said before them, but now they do so in Greek terms. Tatian, for example, tries to show that one cannot possibly regard the sun as a god—as contemporary Greeks did. The sun is a creature of God, something created "for us." The same holds true for the moon and the stars. Using this approach, Tatian gradually tears down all the Greco-Roman gods.

This may seem to be rather innocent play to us, but it entailed great culture shock at that time. Indeed it was a critical and essential moment in the history of the Church, for Judaeo-Christian thought met hellenic thought head on and criticized its very foundations, its "ethico-mythic nucleus." The fundamental values of the Greco-Roman world were gradually undermined until no one believed in them any more. People ceased to live in the Greco-Roman worldview. In 529 B.C. Justinian closed the Platonic Academy in Athens, sounding the death knell of hellenic thought as *an existential, lived reality,* as something which real people believed and lived.

The reason that hellenic thought as living belief died out was the thoroughgoing criticism of the apologists. This fact is of great interest and relevance to us as Latin Americans because a similiar process has not taken place here. Living within the culture of Greece and Rome, Christians transformed that culture by changing the shape and import of its ultimate values. A similar process did not happen here because the native Indians—the Aztecs, the Incas, the Calchaquis—did not have apologists. There were no people living within these native cultures who had grasped and lived their values in such a way that they could change their world for a new one without having to abandon their own civilization. The Amerindian cultures had not evolved to the point where people could make such a transition, "passing over" from one culture to another in this way.

The apologist is a person who is in the *world* and transforms it. This is the first and primary tenet of any mission, even today. But this could not occur in the case of our native Indians. Instead things were "imposed" on them "from above." The name San Salvador was imposed on the name Guanahani, and the latter name simply disappeared. In the era of ancient Roman dominance, by contrast, it was really the autochthonous people and their world that grew into being Christian.

## HISTORY IS FORGOTTEN

The task of the apologist was to gradually trans-form his culture from "within." In the hellenistic empire the apologist was surrounded with a whole panoply of logical tools.[3] But gradually the historical dimension of theological thought was forgotten; theology became more and more a kind of logical argumentation.

In his *Strōmata,* Clement of Alexandria talks very explicitly about this science (Greek *epistēmē*) that he wants to put together. He has in mind a type of reflection that will be on the level of scientific knowledge, that will be Aristotelian in cast. It is to be a theology based on logical argumentation. It starts out with reflection on first principles; this is followed by logical argument which leads to a theological conclusion. Thus people begin to bypass and overlook the kind of theological reflection which takes history as its point of departure.

To be sure, reflection on history is not abandoned completely. Now, however, it is not really on the theological level any more; it is simply a commentary on Scripture. Such commentaries on Scripture now begin to proliferate alongside theological tracts of a logical cast. What remains of historical reflection in theology is to be found in the scriptural commentaries. During the Middle Ages, the latter become so scholastic that they lose all sense of history. The biblical commentaries of Saint Augustine, however, are an important exception to the general trend.

Above I mentioned Clement of Alexandria and his desire to fashion a Christian *epistēmē*, but he is not the first to start this tradition. Irenaeus, Bishop of Lyons, was the first major theologian to propound a systematic theology based on the model of Greek logic. Gradually the Christian sense of history was lost, and so was the Christian sense of prophecy. I remember talking to Père Pierre Benoit in Jerusalem one day. He said to me that the scriptural exegetes are the prophets of today, because they are the ones who are interpreting the word of God *today*. But I think this view is very limited, reducing prophecy to something much less than it really is. The prophet does not simply interpret the "written word"; he also must interpret present history, the "word as lived today." The exegete simply tries to become acquainted with God's "written word"—up to the first century A.D. But doesn't the history of God's people continue after that? Doesn't it remain as real and lofty as it was before? Isn't Jesus still present in his Church through his Spirit?

The sacred history of God's people and the "written word" of the New Testament have their continuation in the history of the Church, and exegesis of Church history is a task incumbent on the prophet. The prophet is the prototype of the Church historian. It is he who discovers the *sense and meaning* of the present—not on the basis of some "happening" but on the basis of faith and its logic, that is, on the basis of the revelation that God grants us about history, about here-and-now history.

When this prophetic sense is lost, all one can do is engage in philological exegesis of the Bible. At the same time theology becomes more and more a process of ratiocination. Attention is focused on the inner coherence of dogma; all its parts have to fit together logically and consistently. But this may easily lead to mere logicizing, and in fact it did. The various facets of a statement or argument may be perfectly coherent and consistent, but sidestep or overlook reality completely. Today, for example, there is a brand of geometry that is non-Euclidean. It "operates" perfectly without in any way being "real." The same approach has sometimes occurred in theology. Taking over certain axioms from the past, axioms which had a very different sense and import in that past, we have fashioned a whole panoply of theological argumentation that leaves present reality completely to one side.

The prophet is a person who "touches" or "puts his finger on" here-and-now reality. He takes it as the point of departure for further reflection. The theologian, on the other hand, may get tied up in his crystal ball and fall prey to merely abstract logicizing, somewhat in the manner of Hegel. Hegel propounds his view of the world process and absolute spirit in a system that is logically coherent but unreal. In like manner a theologian may analyze the various facets of the Old and New Testament in an axiomatic way which strips them of all historical import and reduces them to hellenistic logicizing.

That tendency is now on the wane. But you should see how biblical texts were used by theologians right up to recent times. Scriptural verses were turned into first principles for a theology that was totally out of touch with reality, that showed no interest in history or the task of prophecy. Concrete history, which should have served as the starting point, was confined to the realm of hagiography. The end result in that realm was stereotyped accounts of the lives of the saints.

In the Middle Ages, then, we find little more than anecdotal history. Historical chronicles reported when a certain convent or bishopric was founded. Alongside these chronicles, we find various accounts of the lives of the saints riddled with fantasy and myth and totally out of touch with reality; they completely lacked any *fundamentum in re.*

## CHURCH HISTORY BECOMES
## MERELY PROFANE HISTORY

Christian culture as a whole came to lose touch with reality more and more; and at the same time, paradoxical as it may seem, its history became more and more identical with profane history. This is because it could not help but be profane history insofar as it ceased to be sacred history.

The process of secularization began as far back as the eleventh or twelfth century after Christ, in the dispute over investiture. It gradually gave rise to written history that was profane in nature and that had little to do with the history of the Church. Ecclesial problems were gradually left out of written Church history so that it ceased to be sacred history. By the end of the nineteenth century, the only kind of history to be found was profane history. Whether they realized what they were doing or not, those who chose to keep writing Church history actually ended up writing a secular depiction of that history. They narrated the history of the "institutional Church" as one would narrate the history of any institution. They treated such questions as these: Did Saint Paul get to Spain? If he did, in what year did he arrive? Did Boyl have a certain papal bull when he reached the court of Isabella or not? Did he try to work against Christopher Columbus or not? In short, their histories are merely secular recountings and descriptions of events; yet they pretend to be Church history. The few histories of the Church in Latin America which are in print are almost entirely of this cast.

That should not be the case, because history is the concrete locale, the horizon and *locus,* the *ubi* and source, of theology. Without history there is no theology; history is the starting point and end point for the abstract conceptualizing of theology. This history must of course be something more than merely anecdotal. It must be sacred history, liberation history. The past, from the time of Abraham to today, must have *meaning* in the present so that it can provide an eschatological thrust towards the future. It is history understood in this sense which is the real and preeminent *locus* of theology.

## LACK OF ROOTS AND ALIENATION

When a nation or a people is not familiar with the evolution of its community, when it does not know how it fits into the history that goes back to the beginnings of Christianity, then its theologizing is unreal. Theologians will only alienate those who study under them, propounding notions that are current in Japan or Europe or North America but that don't "work" here. Once we realize that these notions do not work here, we turn to sociology. We will do "religious sociology," we say to ourselves. But that won't work either. Such "religious sociology" often remains at the level of mere statistics. It is not really sociology; it is sociography. In other words, it stops at the level of description and does not explore or explain reality in depth. For an in-depth study and explanation of reality, we must appeal to the human sciences as a whole; we must include economics and politics. We must appeal to the whole history of a culture. When this history is reconsidered in the light of faith, then we are beginning to theologize, to work out a theology of the present moment in history.

Theologians today are well aware of the fact that history is the privileged *locus* of theology. In Europe, for example, this is taken for granted; it is quite normal and logical. The European theologian is solidly integrated and rooted in history, whether he adverts to the fact or not. Such is not the case, however, in Latin America.

Here I do not intend to give an anecdotal account of the facts of Church history in Latin America. Instead I shall try to contemplate and explicitate the meaning and import of certain facts and events. These particular facts and events will serve as the starting point for my theologizing. That is precisely what I will be doing when I try to ponder the meaning of historical facts and events. And when I sum up in my concluding remarks, I will be repeating myself to a certain extent. For the initial exposition itself will provide us with a theological interpretation.

## TOWARDS A LATIN AMERICAN THEOLOGY

A Latin American theology can appear on the scene only after we have tried to comprehend our day-to-day life in history. This would include our economic, political, and cultural life. It is from this that theology arises. Europeans have always been formulating a European theology, a theology which takes everyday life in Europe as its starting point. We Latin Americans have merely aped that theology, alienating ourselves in the process. Only recently have we turned our attention back to our own real life here, discovering a history that has lain buried in obscurity since the sixteenth century. Once again theology has become a real possibility in Latin America, and that in itself is cause for rejoicing.

It was only in 1968 that the first Latin American theological texts began to appear. When I say "Latin American" here, I mean that these texts contain reflections that are peculiar to this segment of the Church and that are different from the thinking of other segments of the Church. Our thinking is so different, in fact, that theologians from other parts of the world do not understand it when we try to explain it to them; sometimes they do not feel it is any concern of theirs at all. In Quito I had a conversation with a German theologian. I was telling him that we were now reflecting on the whole matter of liberation. He expressed surprise and interest, and he asked me to tell him more about it. But do you know what was really on the top of his mind at the moment? Hans Kung's book on papal infallibility. The problem of liberation that occupies us right now was far from his thoughts. Europeans are down to splitting hairs while we must find out whether we even possess a head of hair; and if we do, we must find out how to help it grow.

In short, the situation is very different in the two cases. They are already at the point of engaging in tired subtleties while we are at the point of dawning awareness and new beginnings. Marcuse, for example, is now asking how one can get people in affluent societies to eat less. We are trying to figure out how to make sure that starving people get enough to eat. It seems to me that the person who is desperately trying to find enough food has more passion and enthusiasm in his quest than the person who is beginning to eat less without knowing exactly why. The hippy movement is a rebellious movement within the affluent society. Our rebelliousness is quite different, and it is much more meaningful. Mankind is able to express itself much more completely and much more spiritually in the movements that now mark Latin America, Africa, and Asia than it can in the movements that mark affluent societies.

I shall go into this matter more fully as we proceed. Right now the point is that if we manage to recover our own past history, we will find ourselves with a new and different way of looking at things. Our point of view and our thought will necessarily be quite different from, or even opposed to, the viewpoint and thinking of people in dominant countries such as France, Germany, Italy, Belgium, and the United States. Our questions and problems mean little to them. They will show an interest in hearing from us only when we take the trouble to ponder our own reality. Only then will they begin to respect us as theologians and as a Church, according us some of the rights that go with adulthood. The Latin American Church must find out what mission is properly its own in the near future. It cannot permit other segments of the Church to point out its road to it.

In 1969 a layman wrote a critical article about Cardinal Suenens in the periodical *Víspera* (Methol Ferré,"Crítica a Suenens desde América latina," *Víspera,* no. 12, 1969, Montevideo). His criticism of certain statements by the great Belgian Cardinal can be summarized briefly. Ferré maintains that underlying Suenen's words is a whole world which is not the world of the Latin American. Hence the conclusions drawn by Suenens are ones with which a Latin American cannot agree at all. There are two different theologies involved because there are two different cultural worlds involved and two different political backgrounds.

This article by Ferré heralded the start of autonomous theological thinking on the part of Latin Americans. Although Columbus arrived in the new world in 1492, we might well be justified in saying that we are just beginning to "discover" America—Latin America, in particular. The statement is not as absurd as it might seem at first glance. A child grows up slowly. It does not really discover its self until sometime around adolescence. Only then does it realize that it is "other" than its parents. That is why the adolescent begins to show rebelliousness.

The discovery of self goes hand in hand with the initial steps towards full adulthood. The human individual now realizes that he or she is a new and novel being, and has been such from the very start. In the last couple of decades we have come to realize that our culture is distinct from every other culture. "From the very start," for us, means from the start of our history in 1492. Our mother is Amerindia, our father is Spain—or vice versa, if you will. But the child of this union is something *new*. It is not the culture of Amerindia, Spain, or Europe; nor is it the culture of the Incas or the Aztecs. It is a new culture, a mixed culture, a creole or mestizo culture.

A child is not its mother or its father. But while it is being brought up, it is very much the same as its father or mother. It discovers its distinctness only when it attains its independence. That is what is happening to us today. Discovering ourselves to be an "other," we are turning our eyes back to the past and beginning to discover our own history. That is why we could not really have had a written history of our own before this. One must first discover his own otherness before he can really begin to explore who he is and what his past means.

The existing histories of the "universal" Church are not histories of the "universal" Church at all. If you don't believe me, read what they have to say about Latin America. There is a history of the Church in twenty volumes published under the direction of Augustin Fliche and Victor Martin; it is in French. Latin America is discussed in brief appendices to various chapters, which were written by my professor at the Sorbonne, Robert Ricard. He simply was not able to consider our historical process in its totality, so it is reduced to a missionary adjunct. But the fact is that the Latin American Church is not simply a mission Church. It has its own distinctive institutions. As we shall see, it is a colonial version of Christendom with its own peculiar and distinctive features. It deserves more than an appendix in Church history.

The existing histories of the "universal" Church are really histories of the European Church for the most part. Little or nothing is said in them about Latin America. We cannot comprehend ourselves in these histories because they do not see us as distinct. It is only when we discover we are outside history that we can ask ourselves who we really are. Only then can we turn our gaze back to the beginning of our history and thereby interpret our life here and now. This process is already a process of theologizing, and it cannot help but be Latin American in nature. It will be different because we will be pondering things from a historical perspective that has not been taken into account before.

Whether they now really want that role or not, Europeans have been assigned the role and the responsibility of being the dominating people in the unfolding scheme of world history. It is they who discovered the other "ecumenes" and who gained domination over them by technology, force of arms, and the impact of horses, gunpowder, and caravels. This domination led them to ponder reality from the standpoint of domination, even where theology was concerned. But if we start to ponder things from the other end, from the standpoint of those dominated, then we see everything in a very different light. The theology formulated from the standpoint of the Hebrew slaves in Egypt was hardly akin to that formulated by the pharaoh and his priests.

So we soon find ourselves facing a new horizon and a whole new set of issues. Everything shows up in a very different light, as I shall try to show later. When we recover our past history, we will have a solid foothold for undertaking a new and innovative line of thought. The result will necessarily be new because we ourselves are something new whether we wish to be or not. We will have to explore this newness and see what it is all about. We cannot ask Europeans to explain the meaning of what has happened to us; instead we must explain to them what has happened to us and what it all means. Indeed, it is my opinion that we may be able to see a great deal more clearly from our standpoint here. Looking at things "from the bottom," we may well be able to see more clearly into the universal human condition and to determine which human project should capture the attention of Europeans and others in the near future.

Consider the pharaoh and the Hebrews seeking freedom. Which party possessed the life and vitality that would move the process of liberation forward? Which party would move history further on into the future? The answer is clear. The Hebrews, in their quest for liberation, would give new life and impetus to history and its forward movement. It is they who were the critical factor in history at that moment. That may be true of us today. Living in a situation of oppression, we may be destined to find a way out for the universal Church. We live in a privileged situation: "Blessed are the poor." We are poor. The poor, living in the desert, have fewer possessions to clog up their ears. They are better able to hear the divine message that calls forth and summons onward. They "comprehend" the oppressor and realize that they themselves are oppressed. The oppressor, by contrast, "comprehends" only himself and gags the oppressed. In the last analysis, he does not comprehend anything at all. It may well be that our Latin American theology will prove to be very important, that it will not only reflect on our own situation but also explain a great deal more than European theology does.

Such is my belief, although I have only offered a few general remarks so far. In the words that follow, I shall try to show that I am not dealing in vague, unfounded hypotheses, that there is something to what I have been saying.

## NOTES

1. See my book, *Para una ética de la liberación latinoamericana,* vol. 2, chapter 6, the section on the "método analéctico."

2. Original French edition published by Neuchatel-Delachaux; English translation, *Christ and Time* (Philadelphia: Westminster, 1950).

3. A philosophy seminar on this question, the adoption of hellenic logic and its instrumentation by Christian thought, was held at the Universtiy of Cuyo during the first semester of 1968. See my *El dualismo en la antropología de la Cristiandad* (Buenos Aires: Guadalupe, 1974). It treats this problem in greater detail.

# 2

# Major Stages of World
# and Church History

Here I should like to situate the history of the Latin American Church in a broader context, so that we may be able to get a clearer glimpse of our place as Latin Americans in world history. One of the weak points in our cultural life is that we do not realize the extent to which we are absent from this history. Hence we do not really know what role we might possibly play within it, and what it means to be Latin American Christians in the context of world history.

I shall allude to many different matters in very summary fashion. A truly adequate discussion of them would take much more time than is available here. My desire is to provide an overall sketch of the general context in which our present topics are framed.

THE ORIGINS OF MAN

If we want to interpret the place and role of Latin America in world history, we must begin at the beginning. And the beginning in question here is the very beginning of mankind itself. Starting there, we would have to consider the growth and evolution of humanity as a whole in order to be able to explore the place of our own continent and culture within that story. Only then can we probe the present con-

37

figuration of our culture and determine what role falls to us in the near future.

Right from the start we are confronted with interesting and relevant theological questions which I cannot treat in detail here. Consider the whole matter of "the appearance of man." It is certain that mankind arose from within the animal kindgom. From within the class known as mammals there arose the insectivores. The latter gave rise to the primates, and man developed out of that group. *Homo* transformed the magnificent pageant of biological evolution into history, and God's revelation arose within this history. Divine revelation in history is continued in the history of Latin America too.

If we want to relate our faith to the universe, we must look at the whole ensemble of creation. Only then will we be able to relate our faith to the distant galaxies, intergalactic space, the sun and the solar system, and the animals who frequent the jungle or our fields and city streets. We do not know the precise date when our universe came into existence. It now seems fairly certain that the galaxies expanded from some point. Our own galaxy, for example, is 100,000 light years in diameter and 5,000 light years in depth at its center, having the shape of a plate. That is the "home" in which we live. There are millions of galaxies, the nearest ones to ours being at least a million and a half light years away. In this vast expanse, the solar system is a tiny section. Some five billion years ago the earth solidified within the solar system, setting the stage for the next advance.

It now seems that life appeared on earth some three or three-and-a-half billion years ago. The appearance of life marked a new stage in the whole process of creation, and life too underwent evolution. One-celled organisms were followed by multicelled organisms. In their groping, the latter "discovered" the vegetable kingdom; the animal kingdom developed as a parasite out of the vegetable kingdom. The exploratory groping of the animal kingdom led to the discovery of various possibilities: first there were the insects, later the vertebrates. The members of this subphylum found many different ways to reproduce. One class came to nourish its young on nutrient fluids generated by the female. Within this class, known as the mammals, are such insectivores as the anteater. About seventy million years ago the tarsiers, members of the insectivore group, paved the way for the first true primates. From the higher primates there developed the first beings we now label *homo*. As far as we can tell at present, the latter genus appeared on the scene somewhere around two million years ago. One of the oldest fossils of this genus is that of *homo habilis,* a tool-making creature. So we are dealing with a creature that had fashioned something of a culture, because it had altered its environment to some extent.

Here we encounter a topic that is most interesting and that would deserve a whole book in itself. It certainly would be worthwhile to consider the fact that it is a metaphysics of creation which provides the underpinning for a theory of evolution; evolutionism could appear on the scene only through Judaeo-Christianity. Another interesting question is how God might have created man within the evolutionary process. Such an event is quite possible, as Xavier Zubiri has tried to show in a recent article ("El origen del hombre," in *Revista de Occidente,* no. 17, 1964). When primates had attained the cranial capacity required for reflective thinking—that is, the millions of nerve cells necessary for such an operation—God could have created the "mark" of intelligence intrinsically within man, within the evolutionary process itself. There is evolution because the will of God chose to be evolutionary in its approach.

I do not want to get sidetracked into a long discussion of this particular subject. But it is important if we are to be able to dialogue with our world. Just remember all the false problems we raise in the Church with regard to evolutionary thought. We never seem to advert to the fact that the Greeks believed the world was eternal because it was divine. The cosmos had to be desacralized before it could be regarded as a creature, as a created reality whose species had a definite origin and starting point. Only such a viewpoint could lead people to realize eventually that the origin of species entailed a process of evolution, that species were not divine as the Greeks had thought. Darwin, then, is a product of Christianity; yet we Christians repudiated him as a pagan. It is one of those strange contradictions in which history abounds, and I want to point it out here even though I cannot explore the issue more deeply.

The further evolution of the genus *homo* can be represented as a flowering tree of human life. Proceeding through various forms, we ultimately arrive at *homo sapiens.* This species may have appeared around two hundred thousand years ago. Today all human beings are members of the species *homo sapiens.* With the appearance of *homo sapiens,* the whole evolution of the cosmos is concretized in an unfolding process which we call history. The life of *homo sapiens* today is part of the two-million year history of man's presence on this earth.

NEOLITHIC CULTURE

The first period of man's cultural life is known as the paleolithic. It is the vast expanse of time when man shaped stone into rough but useful tools. Leaving aside that period, we can say that there have been three basic cultural stages in world history which will help us to appreciate the place and situation of Latin America within that history. The first stage is the neolithic period and the rise of the first great civilizations. The second stage is the invasion of the Indo-European cultural groups. The third stage is the invasion of the Semitic peoples. I shall now discuss these three periods, but I ask the reader to remember that I am not talking about a chronological order of events but about a series of events that had major cultural impact.

The first stage, then, is the period of neolothic culture. It entailed a great urban revolution. Thanks to the development of agriculture and the domestication of animals, man could settle down in groups and live in towns. The division of labor became possible and grew in complexity. This led to further progress, and eventually to the rise of large urban centers and the first great cultures or civilizations.

The first great civilization arose in lower Mesopotamia, on the Persian Gulf, around the fourth millenium before Christ. The second great civilization arose in Egypt around the start of the third millenium. Thus it was not just mere chance that a man named Abraham would set out from the city of Ur, or that his descendants would find themselves in Egypt. Israel lived its life between these two great centers of civilization, the two oldest centers of world history. Israel's life is *rooted in history,* even as the life of Jesus would be later on. The Israelites would always remain a very poor people, but they would undergo intense cultural evolution because they lived between the two oldest civilizations of mankind. The fact is undeniable.

The third great culture appeared in the Indus Valley around 2500 B.C. The fourth appeared on the Yellow River about 1500 B.C. By contrast, the last two civilizations to be mentioned here appeared on the American continent. The Mayan-Aztec civilization flourished after the time of Jesus Christ; its classical period is dated from 300 to 900 A.D., when the great city of Teotihuacán was a cultural center. The classic period of Inca civilization, with its great center at Tiahuanaco, was contemporaneous with that of the Mayan-Aztec civilization.

These six civilizations are the great cultural pillars which will enable us to understand world history. Five thousand years separate the start of Mesopotamian civilization from the rise of the American civilizations. The cultural process

moves from East to West, and our prehistory is centered on
the Pacific Ocean. Needless to say, the Incas and the Aztecs
were not the only groups involved in our cultural history.
There were the Chibchas in Colombia, the various Indian
cultures of North America, and other groups besides. But
the overall configuration of our *prehistory,* which includes
the existence of two great civilizations, will help to explain
our *history.*

We must realize that conquering the Incas was not the
same thing as "pacifying" nomadic tribes of Indians. The
conquest of a great center such as Cuzco meant the conquest of an empire containing millions of people. By contrast, the nomadic tribes of North and South America were
never really conquered. The European newcomers to
North America moved forward slowly, killing Indians as
they went. General Roca did the same thing in Argentina as
he pushed forward with the "conquest of the desert." We
should not imagine that the story of English settlement is
one of complete malice while the story of Spanish settlement is one of sweetness and light. Prehistoric factors help
to explain why the method of conquest in the two cases was
different, even though they may not justify the method
used.

### The Aztec Worldview

War was an essential element in the ethos or *Weltanschauung*
of the Aztecs. They were a warrior people by nature, and
this tendency found expression in their cult of the sun.
Intermingled in this cult were elements borrowed from the
agricultural peoples of the valley and from the primitive
hunters of the north whence the Nahua people came. The
uranic element was not only united with the sun but also
intermingled with various animals. Such is the case with the
gods worshipped at the great temple in Tenochtitlán. This
temple was dedicated principally to *Huitzilopochtli.* He had

originally been the tribal god of the Aztecs, the god of the "daytime sky." But he was transformed into a "god of war" who came to counsel his people in the form of a humming-bird (animal epiphany), a hummingbird armed with shield, darts, and propellant. *Tonatiuh*—the sun—was the chief god of the firmament. *Huitzilopochtli* and *Tezcolipoca* (the god of the nightime sky) were his incarnations.

There was also a uranic god in the proper sense of the term, but only the city of Tezcoco had a conscious cult to him. This uranic god, *Tloque Nahuaque,* was the creator and source of everything in existence—even prior to the dual gods *Tonacatecuhtli* and *Tonacacihuatl.* A more humble position was held by *Quetzalcoatl* (the "plumed serpent"), who was the god of wisdom, the priesthood, the wind, the planet Venus, and the setting sun.

Chthonic elements were assimilated belatedly, and they retain a negative cast. *Tlaltecuhtli* ("Lord of the earth") and *Coatlicúe* ("Mother Earth") are represented as a monstrous and fiercesome amphibian animal.

All this suggests the primacy of the hunter and warrior in

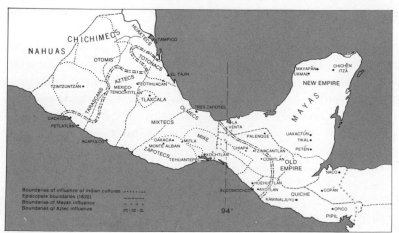

HIGHER CULTURES OF THE MAYAN-AZTEC AREA

this culture, and the mentality of the mercenary or the soldier of fortune. It was these people who held sway over the sedentary groups and effected a certain measure of symbiosis by syncretizing various elements, without achieving the degree of unity visible in the cultures of Eurasia or Africa. Uranic and chthonic elements were syncretized by hunting peoples who were gradually changing their way of life and settling down as agriculturalists. The short duration of the Aztec empire enables us to see that it was a culture which was still at an embryonic stage but evolving steadily; it had not yet attained complete maturity when the Spaniards arrived.

A characteristic feature in the primitive mentality is quite evident among the Aztecs: namely, the a-historicity of human existence. The "Great Year" and the repetition of creation are themes which underlie the developing theology proposed by the priesthood in the Aztec empire. To this must be added belief in the predestination that applies to every life. This belief and its attendant rites produced familiar effects: concrete existence was elevated to the realm of the sacred. Every action was lived out in "mythical time," being a repetition of the archetypal sacred action performed by the gods.

Three categories of people possessed life in "the beyond": the warrior slain in battle, the victim sacrificed to the gods, and the woman who died in childbirth. All three were made equal to the gods, or at the very least immortalized as companions of the Sun, since the Sun was the first paradise. The conquistadores were horrified by human sacrifice, regarding it as an offense against human dignity. In fact, however, it signified a false exaltation of the human person based on a faulty appreciation of divine dignity. Mircea Eliade points up the deeper underlying motif: "To find the meaning of these human sacrifices we must look into the primitive theory of the seasonal regeneration of the forces of the sacred . . . . A regeneration sacrifice is a ritual "repetition" of the Creation. The myth of creation includes the ritual (that is, violent) death of a primeval giant, from whose body the worlds were made, and plants grew . . . . The object in sacrificing a human victim for the regeneration of the force expressed in the harvest is to repeat the act of creation that first made grain to live. *The ritual makes creation over again* . . . . "[1] The mythical scheme is identical whether we are dealing with the creation of the cosmos, of all humanity, of a particular race of people, or of other species. Nothing can be created without immolation. Sacrifice brings about an awesome transference in which the life concentrated in one person is diffused to others, manifesting itself on a collective or even cosmic scale.

When the Aztecs ate the flesh of a victim who had undergone voluntary self-immolation, they were eating the flesh of a god because the victim was apotheosized. Not only were they gaining a hold over the will of the gods, they were actually ensuring the existence of the gods, the world, and the human race. It was not simply a matter of ensuring their military power and supremacy; it was a matter of ensuring the continuance of cosmic and biological existence. A typical instance was the annual feast to the god *Tezcalipoca*. A similar outlook is evident in the pilgrimage which took place at the end of each "Great Year" (comprising fifty-two solar years). The people journeyed to the "hill of the star" near Colhuacán. At night, after all the fires of the land had been extinguished, they sought to light the "new fire" over the blood of a victim. If the priests succeeded, it meant that the gods would grant cosmic and biological existence for another period of fifty-two solar years. In orgiastic revelry the "new fire" was distributed throughout the region. It was the divine fire symbolizing and ensuring heat and life.

The monuments and documents left behind by this civilization give us a glimpse into the cosmic "home" which the Nahuatl peoples fashioned for themselves. The key to their symbolic world is to be found in their ancient myths, in their religious doctrines, and in the thinking of their sages, the *tlamantinime*. We cannot go into great detail about the beliefs and doctrines of the Aztec world, which indicate some first steps towards self-conscious rationalizing. Here I shall merely allude to four *tlamatinime* whose thinking indicates certain basic elements in the Toltec and Aztec vision of the cosmos. All four are historical personages. They deserve the same study and attention that is now accorded to such figures as the pre-Socratic thinkers.

*Quetzalcoatl* (9th century A.D.), a solitary young man from the region of Tulancingo, was sought out by the people of Tula. He became their governor, wise man, and priest; and he was also the first great Toltec thinker. He taught that the world was an immense island horizontally divided into four directions, with a navel at its center. The east was the region of light, fertility, and life—symbolized by the color white. The west was the home of the sun, symbolized by the color red. The north was the land of the dead, symbolized by the color black. The south was the region of seedland, symbolized by the color blue. Above the earth was the blue sky which was formed by all the waters and in which the sun, moon, and stars travelled along their paths. Below the earth was Mictlán, the realm of the dead. This world, filled with gods and invisible forces, had existed on and off four different times. In their cosmogonic battles the gods produced different periods or ages of the world, each age coming to an end in a cataclysmic upheaval. The present age was the age of the "sun in motion," and the chief god was Ometéotl, the god of duality. As a Toltec poem expresses it:

> The Toltecs knew quite well that there are many heavens,
> that there are twelve divisions superimposed above
> where lives the true god and his consort,
> the celestial god, the Lord of Duality.

This great sage gave form and structure to the whole complex of Toltec wisdom (*Toltecáyotl*), which would be idealized in later ages:

*The Toltecs were wise people.*
*Toltecáyotl, the whole body of their arts*
*and wisdom, came from Quetzalcoatl . . . .*
*The Toltecs were very rich and happy . . . .*

The most well-known of the Nahua *tlamatinime,* *Nezahualcóytl,* was born in Tezcoco in 1402. After serving as the leader and ruler of that city, he died in 1472. He may be regarded as a real Solon by virtue of his creativity as a legislator; but he was also a sage thoroughly acquainted with Toltec tradition because he had studied at Calmécac, the educational center for the nobility. Opposing the official ideology of the Aztecs, he had a temple built to Tloque Nahuque, the one god who overcomes change and death. This sage described him as "the one who is fashioning himself" (*Moyocoyatzin*). But it was the tragic contingency of human life that preoccupied this sage:

*Togetherness lasts only for a moment,*
*glory for but a brief period . . . .*
*Your beautiful flowers . . .*
*are nothing but dried-up flowers.*

*Where shall we go*
*that death does not exist?*

Perhaps the sage who had the greatest practical impact was *Tlacaélel,* who was born in 1398. He fashioned a theoretical system that served as the basis for real-life action, and he was the undisputed counselor of the first Aztec king, Itzcoatl. It was he who gave the Aztec empire its mythical, warrior vision of the cosmos. To do this, he rethought all the theogonies of the valley area. All the codices of opposing groups, those of the city of Azcapotzalco in particular, were burned. The utmost unity was needed to weld the Aztec empire together; to integrate its religious, economic, educational, military, and socio-political life. Huitzilopochtli, a forgotten god, would now take first place.

This god of war was born as the son of Coatlicúe on the "Mountain of the Serpent." It was he who led the Mexica-Aztecs through the northern plains to Lake Tezcoco. While this sage modified earlier traditions, he took great care to provide continuity with Toltec tradition also. Thus he made Huitzilopochtli the god who presides over the age of the Sun in motion. In fact, this god was the Sun itself. If he died, the fifth age of the world would come to a catastrophic end. To get back the vital energy he needed, this god had to have blood. Blood was the "precious water" (*chalchíhuatl*) that would restore his vitality. By offering victims to him, the Aztecs carried out a sacred and important duty. Their battles were sacred functions, their wars were "holy wars." In short, Tlacaélel worked out a whole theology of the Aztec military conquest:

> *This is the office of Huitzilopochtli,*
> *our God.*
> *For this has he come. To bring into his service*
> *all the nations*
> *by the strength of his brave breast and head.*

The fourth *tlamatinime* we shall mention here was *Tecayehuatzin*. He ruled Huexotzinco around 1501. He might well be regarded as the sage of Nahuatl poetry, symbol, and speech.

### The Inca Worldview

The principal divinity of the Inca empire was called different names at different points in history. In an earlier period the people of the coastal area had called him *Pachacamac,* but later the Incas called him *Huiracocha* (or *Viracocha*). This creator god, too, was a product of syncretism. We must remember that the Incas cannot be viewed as a non-specialized people. Nor were they simply hunters or herdsmen. They were a settled, sedentary civilization with a highly developed culture.

Uranic religions—that is, religions with sky gods—are typical of non-specialized peoples or peoples at an early stage of development. Their limited supply of tools and their freedom with respect to nature enables them to evince an attitude of supreme respect for the "heavenly father." This god is a creator god, at least in the sense that he has formed or shaped the world and other gods. *Huiracocha* certainly was the great sky god. In the eyes of the Inca elite he was an abstract, spiritual god who was also present. In

Key

1. MANABI
2. CHANCHAN
3. MOCHE
4. CHAVIN DE NUANTAR
5. RECUAY
6. LIMA
7. PACHACAMAC
8. ICA
9. MACHU PICCHU
10. OLLANTAYTAMBO
11. CUZCO
12. TIAHUANACO

boundaries of the Empire ·+·+·|·+·
episcopate boundaries (1620) ----------

HIGHER CULTURES OF THE PRE-INCA AREA

the eyes of the common folk he was a remote and incomprehensible god. That is why we find so few temples dedicated to this god. Most of them gave way to all sorts of idolatry as the familiar processes of fusion and substitution took place.

There is a tendency for the sacred to undergo a gradual "fall" into the concrete. Various divinities become more dynamic, accessible, and concretely effective. A process of specialization takes place, so that a *deus otiosus,* a god with nothing to do, turns into a *deus pluviosus,* a god of rain or thunder. And thus we get a cult of the sun.

*Inti*—the holy Sun—represents the solarization of the creator. He becomes a fecundating god in a world of stunning and dramatic vegetation. He is also the god of hunters and warriors. Vestiges of theism and animism are intermingled with the political role and funtion of hunter-warriors. The solar ruler becomes the monarchical incarnation of the masculine ideal which dominates a hierarchically ordered civilization.

We are presented with a whole new world when we meet *Quilla* (the moon) and *Pachamama* ("Mother Earth"). Here we find a real counterpart to the theism described above. Sedentary agricultural peoples of a more feminine or matriarchal cast organize their theology around chthonic structures. Here we find animism, manism, and totemism. There is a link among woman, the earth, the moon, fertility, and the rhythmic cycles of biological and cosmic life.

Whereas uranic religions tend to discover the *transcendent god,* chthonic religions tend to interpret *immanent life* in sacral terms. The moon itself is a symbol of this immanent movement of death and rebirth. It "grows" and goes into a "death agony." It "dies" for three days and then is "reborn" to carry out its twenty-eight-day cycle anew. In like manner, the earth and the soil are interpreted as a god or goddess.

The Incas, like the Aztecs, were a higher culture in which there was a great deal of amalgamation or syncretism. Gods from the uranic religions of hunting peoples intermingled with gods or goddesses from the chthonic religions of agricultural peoples. Alongside the sun god of the Inca empire we find the totemic deities of Ayllu.

The idea of *rhythm* is discovered quite early by primitive peoples with a chthonic religion. Rituals and cultic ceremonies enable the community to relive the sacred happenings which the gods live out in an exemplary manner.

The feast of the sun was celebrated on June 22, when the days began to get longer. It was the people's invocation for the gift of a new year. Representatives of the people and the Inca himself gathered in the great plaza of Cuzco. There, in silence, they watched the sun rising above the mountain ranges to the east. The Incas believed that one day the sun would refuse to rise, and that this would mark the end of our world. So when the Sun did rise on that date, the Inca himself offered a juice prepared by consecrated virgins from sacred fruits.

The feast of the moon was celebrated at the start of spring, on September 22. It bears witness to the close relationship among the rebirth of life, the seeded earth as a "mother," and the moon which guides this process of rebirth. For total rebirth, however, pardon was necessary. (In Hebrew the term is *purim*.) The people waited for the moon to appear in the nighttime sky. Then they raised a cry, pleading for the removal of their faults and for the elimination of all threats and dangers. Soldiers set out in pursuit of "evil spirits" while the people proceeded to undergo ablutions for the sake of ritual purification. The gods responded by renewing and purifying the life of the people in town and countryside.

I cannot make a thorough analysis of Inca religion here. I simply want to point out its general features: a complex cultural base; ritual and cultic syncretism; intermingling of uranic and chthonic religious elements; a highly developed religious awareness which brought sacral unity to human

life on every level, from the most private acts of the Inca
and the elite to the most secular manifestations of community life. Anything unforeseen or unexpected, which might
leave room for "the profane" to steal into the picture, was
immediately sacralized upon its appearance. Thus sick
people and premature infants were declared divine and
given special protection—quite in contrast to the sacral
attitude of the Spartans, for example.

Socio-cultural dualism was an indisputable fact in the
Inca empire. The Inca nobility did not adore the sun as a
supreme being; they adored *Huiracocha* or *Pachacamac* with
rites and liturgies of their own. The Great Priest (*amauta* or
*Uillac Umu*) was the head of the most important priestly
institution in the empire. Once a province was conquered,
the cult of the sun was established and a temple was set up in
the most important localities. A local clergy was formed
from among the aristocracy of the conquered people. All
the lands of the empire were divided into various sectors for
administrative purposes; one sector, the sector "of the sun,"
was set aside for temples and the clergy. But priests were
never very numerous.

Among the Aztecs, by contrast, cultic worship utilized a
far greater number of priests. There were more than 5,000
priests in the capital. Two Great Priests were in charge of
the cultic life of the empire. The priestly school, noted for
its strict asceticism, was located in Calmecac.

In Yucatan there was a Great Priest called *Ahaukan Mai;*
his function was hereditary. In the Mayan empire the
members of the priestly class came from the nobility and
performed military functions; they were the *Nacon.* They
must have been behind all the great construction work of
this culture, for the products are temples and cities of
pilgrimage, i.e., religious centers. The name *Ahkin,* which
was given to the common Mayan priest, is now given to the
Catholic priest.

Throughout the major American civilizations, the priesthood was an imperial one. Thus it opposed or restricted the local priesthood (sorcerers, diviners, shamans, and so forth). Given enough time, the imperial priesthood would probably have suppressed the local priesthood almost completely, but it had not imposed its supremacy on the local priesthood when the Spaniards arrived. The disappearance of the Indian empires inevitably led to the rebirth of local idolatry. The Spanish Church, recently organized itself, did not realize exactly what was taking place.

For its part, the indigenous civilization was unable to dialogue with the new invaders. It had not reached the stage where it could rationalize or justify its "mythical world" adequately. We now know that philosophy did not originate in psychological "wonder." (Perhaps we should say "theology" rather than "philosophy," since the latter, as a rational science reduced to the study of non-divine things, is of recent vintage.) Its origin is to be sought in a historical fact which is easily verifiable, namely, the incomprehension of the hellenic elite when faced with the conflict or contradiction between the primitive mythical tradition of Crete and the Mediterranean on the one hand and the Indo-European mythical tradition imported by the Acheans and Dorians.

The process of rationalization had only begun among the Incas, the Aztecs, and the Mayans. The Mexican priests, for example, were trying to bring a little order into the chaotic welter of myths which stemmed from different sources. Thus they reduced the chief gods to four, corresponding to the four cardinal points and deriving their descent directly from the primordial pair. But such rationalizations were scarcely accepted by everyone, and they even contradicted other myths that were still very much alive—such as the various myths about mother goddesses. Religion was predominantly a local, folk affair, as Toynbee suggests, and theological rationalization played a minimal role.

## THE INDO-EUROPEANS

A second cultural stage occurred when a series of invasions from the north swept over the Eurasian continent during the second millenium before Christ. Gradually the existing original cultures were submerged totally under alien domination. These aliens were the Indo-Europeans.[2]

Around 4000 B.C. the Indo-Europeans lived somewhere north of the Black Sea and the Caspian Sea. Their original homeland was the Eurasian steppe area. The first to domesticate the horse, they were skillful riders and roamed from Chinese Turkestan to Spain. In successive waves they invaded the richer regions to the south.

The first great Indo-European invasion was that of the Hittites, who possessed a real empire in the second millenium. Other Indo-European groups went into Europe—e.g., the Celts, the Italic tribes, and the various groups that invaded Greece. Still other Indo-European groups were the Medes, the Persians, and the Aryans who invaded India in the fifteenth century B.C.

These peoples had a *worldview* of their own. Features of this view can be deduced from various elements in the vocabulary of their languages. But this is not the precise area that is of interest to us here. I simply would like to consider four aspects in their mentality and outlook on the world.

### Anthropological Dualism

First, in almost all these peoples we find a view of man that is always dualistic in one way or another. For all these peoples, the body is somehow a "prison" or "mere appearance" (*maya*) or something negative. For the Manicheans, it was the root of sin. The view of the body as a prison can be found among the Greeks: *sōma/sēma*. Among the Hindus, the body is mere appearance or *maya*. Among the Iranians, the body was something evil; and from them would come Manicheanism.

In other words Greece, Persia, and India were focal points of Indo-European cultures, and they all possessed an anthropology that was in some way dualistic. Someone might interject here that men such as Aristotle got beyond this dualism, and I would certainly agree that Aristotle did "to a degree." But it cannot be denied that the outlook of a cultural world is predetermined to some extent by its history, even though men of genius may get beyond this influence by looking closely at reality and then challenging the *a priori* ideas of their people. Aristotle may have done this, but unfortunately those who came after him fell back into dualism. This dualism reached its culmination in Plotinus, who represents the synthesis of all the Indo-European cultures.

## Moral Dualism

This dualistic anthropology had a determining influence on the *ethos* of these peoples—that is, on their predominant attitudes and views of things. Thus their morality was dualistic too, because the body was a source of evil in one way or another. Hellenic ethics is a process of ascesis, of liberating man from the body so that he can rise towards the values of the spirit and attain contemplation. The Buddhist strives for liberation from the body, even for the destruction of the body, since it multiplies desire; the goal is to lose one's individuality in Brāhman. And just as the body is something negative for Buddha, so it is for the Hindus in a different way. And then there were such groups as the Manicheans, who were later succeeded by the Cathari and the Albigensians. They opposed all bodily contact and physical pleasure; their moral code was against marriage. The body and everything having to do with the senses was evil.

Note that this is a dualistic morality, and that we have accepted this morality, at least to some extent; Manichean morality has had a profound impact on many peoples in the West. The prototype of such a dualistic morality is the morality of the Iranians, because they ontified good and evil by turning them into two principles of being. As they saw it, there were two gods: a god of good and a god of evil. Saint Augustine had to tackle this issue when he wished to get beyond Manicheanism. He would find his solution in another view of the world.

### Ahistoricism

A third element to be studied here is the historical consciousness of the Indo-Europeans. In their eyes real *being*, the divine, was *eternal*. There was no consistency or solidity to the corporeal realities of this world, hence they were subject to generation and corruption. Holding this view, the Indo-Europeans could not discern the *meaning* of history. Deeply imbedded in their consciousness is the doctrine of eternal return. Individual things completely lose their sense of being particular individuals; of necessity they are reabsorbed in an unending process of repetition. In his treatment of the history of religions, Mircea Eliade describes how primitive peoples—and the Indo-European is the last great instance of a primitive people—de-historify everyday happenings. Primitive peoples feel that in each act of everyday life they are repeating the archetypal actions of the gods. If a primitive decides to contract marriage, for example, it is not a personal act; rather, it is an act which imitates the marriage of some god to some goddess. The act of sowing seed is not a personal action; it is the act of a sower god. Thus the actions of everyday life become mere imitations of eternal archetypes. History does not exist because neither the corporeal realm nor history have any real solidity. History is bound up with corporeality and liberty; hence it lacks consistency. Such an outlook is ahistorical.

*Panontic Totality*

For all these peoples, then, the divine is eternal. It is the only reality, the only true being, the Totality. It is the *being* of Parmenides, which stands over against non-being. And so, paradoxically enough, one moves from anthropological dualism towards a monist thrust in ontology. What is, is one. The plural entities in this world of appearances have no real consistency. If any worldview offers a good explanation of this, it is the worldview of the Hindus. If any Indo-European philosophy represents a culmination of this viewpoint, it is the philosophy of Plotinus.

Plotinus lived in Alexandria in the third century A.D. All the great Indo-European currents from the past came together in the Alexandria of that day, and Plotinus gave them paradigmatic expression. Yet as far as I know, there is no book of philosophy which points up this connection among all the Indo-European peoples. It is a task that we have just begun to tackle.

This cultural outlook will have enormous repercussions during the course of time, for many peoples, the Romans and the Celts, for example, will come to share it to some extent. By understanding it, we can gain some insight into the *basic underlying structures* of the whole Indo-European mentality. This mentality evinced scorn for the body, for plurality, and for history: it valued the One, the All, and contemplation. And while this One might be called the divine, it was very different from what we would call God.

*Some Consequences*

The person who held this view of the world believed that the way to attain perfection was to leave the city and lead a *solitary* life of goodness. It was the *solitaria bonitas* of the Romans. Intersubjective relationships took place on the level of corporeal life whereas perfection was to be attained in solitude away from city life. The Platonic sage chose to leave the city, contemplate the divine in solitude, and then come back to tell people how he had arrived at truth. The Aristotle of the *Nichomachean Ethics* (Book X) is also a contemplator of the divine, who makes use of the city to enjoy the benefits of additional but secondary values. Buddha leaves his parents and the city in order to go away and "kill" his desires in solitary contemplation—outside history and community life.

Hence one can justifiably say that this approach is a *flight* from political intersubjectivity designed to ensure the attainment of perfection in solitude. This, in very brief form, is an outline of the Indo-European worldview. In my book on hellenistic humanism I have treated this whole subject in greater detail.

## THE SEMITES

There was another view of man, however. It was found in the third cultural world that I wish to discuss here—the cultural world of the Semites. The cultural outlook of the Semites was radically different from that of the Indo-Europeans. Hence their ethos and their way of using the things of this world were radically different also. I hope to show that the interplay of these two different views forms the backdrop for our own history as Latin Americans. The starting point for our culture does not go back to the independence movements of the early nineteenth century or to the explorations of the sixteenth century. It goes much farther back, to the influences which helped to form the mentality of the European and to fashion the outlook of the Church itself.

The Semites did not originate in the Eurasian steppe area. They came from the Arabian desert region. The first Semites known to history were the Akkadians. (The Sumerians were not Semites.) The Akkadians were followed by many other Semitic peoples—such as the Amorites, the Babylonians, and the Phoenicians. The Semites also include the Hebrews and the Arabs.

At a certain point in history, just before the start of Christianity, we could very well say that the Indo-Europeans had taken control of the situation. The Roman empire dominated in the west, the Persian empire existed in the Near East, and the Hindu empire predominated farther east. Then a revolution occurred. Christianity, which embodies a Semitic view of the world as we shall see, spread all over the Indo-European area. Islam would come later to complete the trend. This cultural transition, I believe, justifies my hypothesis about three cultural stages. As I noted above, we first have six major civilizations. Then the Indo-European outlook gained dominance in the Eurasian world. Finally, the whole area was "semitized" culturally; and our own culture today shows marked traces of this process.

Let us now consider the outlook of the Semites, which differed radically from that of the Indo-Europeans.[3]

## Unitary Anthropology and
## Intersubjective Bipolarity

First of all, the Semites regarded man as a unity. For the Greeks, man was a participation in the divine and the terrestrial. (Aristotle was an exception here.) Man was man by virtue of the *psychē,* the "soul," which was an independent substance or *ousia* in man. The Semites, by contrast, regarded man as a unitary entity. Here we shall use the Hebrews as our example of the Semitic mentality.

Three Hebrew words are relevant here. The word *basar* signified "flesh," "man," or the "totality," not "body" in the Greek sense. The word *nephesh* signified "life" rather than "soul" as we use the term. And the word *ruah* signified the "divine breath" or "spirit."

In the outlook of the Israelites, man was a unity—but a unity totally given in two different orders. One order was that of *basar*, the "flesh," which is translated in the Greek New Testament as *sarx*. The other order, which signified man as a wholly open totality, was that of *ruah;* that term was translated as *pneuma* in the Greek New Testament.

Paul has an interesting discussion of resurrection (1 Cor. 15), which is more easily understood if we appreciate the distinction in Semitic anthropology between *sarx* and *pneuma*. Before the resurrection we have a merely natural or fleshly body, a body in the order of *basar*. After the resurrection we will have a spiritual body, a body that is wholly in the order of *ruah*. The contrast is between two totalities that represent two wholly different ways of living. The fleshly man lives in the closed totality of the created world. The spiritual man lives in the world of the divine spirit; he is open to God and his covenant.

A similar outlook can be found in the Koran, where there is no distinction between body and soul. And the Syrian Fathers of the Church use the terms *basar* and *nephesh* to describe equivalent totalities.

The point I want to make here is that man is viewed as a unified and unitary being in the Hebrew tradition and in the Bible. Where dualistic formulations are evident, as in the book of Wisdom for example, it is hellenic influence that is making itself felt. There one reads comments on the corruptible body and on the soul that separates itself from the body after death.

## An Ethos of Liberty and Liberation

The ethos deriving from this particular understanding of the world was one which ascribed to man in his totality—not merely the body—the responsibility for the evil in the world. The Hebrew worked out a morality of liberty and liberation.

Liberty was not ascribed to the body or the soul as separate entities. It was ascribed to man in his totality as an autonomous being. The myth of Adam attempts to explain the mystery of evil and its origin. This account tells us that evil is not brought about by God, nor is it a god; instead it has its roots in the liberty of man, in the liberty of Adam. Adam is not presented as someone tragically enslaved, but as someone dramatically tempted as a free agent. In the eyes of the Semite, the body was not the root of evil but the root of liberty. Instead of maintaining an ethos of dualistic forces, the Semite followed an ethos of liberty and liberation.

If the reader would like to explore the meaning and deeper import of the myth of Adam, I would recommend that he or she read a book by Paul Ricoeur on the symbolism of evil. He provides a good analysis of the problem of good and evil as described in the book of Genesis.[4] In his analysis he uses the term "myth" in a different sense than Bultmann does; he shows just how myth can be regarded as something reasonable and rational. Symbol, because of its ambivalence, is likewise as important and necessary today in our technological age. Ricoeur tackles this important subject in a later book.[5]

*Perfection as Personal Commitment*
*and Involvement*

A third area where the Semitic outlook differs radically from that of the Indo-European is the area of personal life and the quest for perfection. For the Semite, intersubjectivity is a necessary prerequisite for perfection. Whereas the Greek sought to escape the body and interpersonal relationships in order to attain perfection, the Hebrew saw man as a totality interrelated with other human totalities. Man could be saved only in this intersubjective web of relationships. The Hebrew could not be saved alone, by contemplating the divine in solitude. He could be saved only by belonging to the people of Abraham, sharing the promise and hoping for its fulfillment. The Hebrew felt closely bound up with his forefathers, and ultimately with Abraham: hence the great concern for genealogy in the Old Testament.

Lacking such intersubjectivity, neither the Hebrew nor the Arab Muslim could be saved. Perfection was always a community affair. He had to belong to the *polis,* the "city of God"; in that sense perfection was always a "political" matter. For the Greek, by contrast, perfection was utterly apolitical.

The Greek sage would attain perfection by solitary contemplation. The Semite would attain perfection by active involvement in his community and personal commitment to history. Hence Semitic perfection is the perfection of the *prophet,* who gives his life to the task of liberating the community of the poor and the oppressed. A prophet such as Moses must go and tell his people what God has told him. He is bound to history and to personal involvement. Semitic perfection, then, is personal involvement in the task of liberating the community. The "Servant of Yahweh" (see Isa. 40ff.) must be willing to give up his life for his community.

### Awareness of History

The Greek devalued history because he devalued the concrete realm, seeing that it could not be reduced to some universal formula. The Hebrew restored value to history and, in fact, discovered history and its value. This is what Hegel suggests when he says that self-awareness begins in world history with Abraham. And this is what Mircea Eliade suggests near the end of his fine book, *The Myth of the Eternal Return.* [6]

The Semite, and the Hebrew in particular, made history the horizon of his existence. It is the concrete fact of Abraham's existence that enables his people to be saved. It is that historical promise which provides the context for Hebrew salvation. Abraham is not a myth or a god. He is not Hercules, Prometheus, or Ulysses. Abraham is a historical figure who lived in Ur at one point and then journeyed through the real world.

Concrete realities are suddenly "discovered." For now the corporeal realm of the individual and the unforeseen—*basar*—can be the starting point for salvation. History is now the starting point for salvation. The prophet is the perfect human being because he discovers the import of history, ponders it, and then proclaims it to his people. He tells people how God sees history and mankind's place in it.

This worldview came about because the Semites saw the world as something radically separated from the Creator, the Other. Using the term *barah*, the first verse of Genesis tells us that the creator God fashioned a world that was radically distinct from himself. In other words, the Transcendent de-mythified *this* world and turned it into man's instrument. So long as the world was divine, so long as it was "full of gods," man could not possibly dominate nature. Thanks to the Hebrew view, he can.

The first important step in man's attempt to dominate nature was the de-mythification of the universe. Modern science, as Pierre Duhen observes, is based on the simple principle of a creator God. It is this principle that allowed man to de-mythify the universe and take scientific control over the world. If the moon is something created, then I can go about the task of studying it. But if the moon is a god or goddess, then astronomy becomes mixed up with theology and science becomes impossible. As you can see, the topic is an interesting one which deserves further study.

## THE PHENOMENON OF CHRISTIANITY

Christians appeared on the scene during the third Semitic stage of world cultural history, and they evangelized the Roman empire. Islam, too, is a Semitic phenomenon which spread far and wide. This Semitic history of Europe has been extended down to the age of secularization. In a secularized form it has to be extended even to China, which eventually was won over to a way of thinking that is ontologically Semitic to a certain extent: i.e., Marxism. Thus only one group remains Indo-European still: India and Southeast Asia. All the other groups in the world have been "Semitized," practically speaking.

Christianity, then, appears within the context of this vast cultural process of Semitization. Indeed it appears in the very bosom of Semitic culture. For our purposes here, I shall divide the history of Christianity into three periods and discuss them briefly in this section.

The *first* period is the period of the apostolic community in Palestine. There Jesus founded his Church after teaching his disciples and carrying out his work. The community grew in Jerusalem and Palestine. Eventually some disciples set out for Antioch, and sister Churches were established there and at Corinth.

During this period, which lasts up to about 50 A.D., the group of disciples underwent certain key experiences that would be of great importance for the Church in the future. The disciples in Jerusalem made up what Paul called the "community of saints." Those who went to Antioch underwent a basic and pivotal experience. The Christians at Antioch were people who came both from Judaism and paganism. This was a new experience, not shared by the Jerusalem community. Saint Paul was the prototype of the Antiochean apostle. He was the apostle to the gentiles because Barnabas introduced him to the pastoral approach of the Antiochean community. Corinth was still another type of community. All the people there were pagan in origin, so the Judaizing tendency was not found in its midst.

At the Synod of Jerusalem James presided. But he gave the floor to Peter, who set forth the general lines that would be followed. But it was Paul who imposed his view on the group, and we enter the second main period of Church history.

The *second* period is the one in which Christianity spread all over the Mediterranean world. As is well known, one of the first great crises occurred when a dispute arose between two factions in the Church: the hellenic faction and the Judaizing faction. When the synod was held in Jerusalem around 49 or 50 A.D., the maturing consciousness of the apostles brought them to the realization that Christianity could not be confined to Jewish people, that it had to be open to the hellenic world and the culture of the Mediterranean world. A new period in Church history had begun.

This period runs from 50 A.D. to 1962, covering almost two thousand years. During this period Christians evangelized the Mediterranean area, and a Christianized Mediterranean remained the fundamental base and site of Christianity for this long period of time. During this period Christians also evangelized the eastern Roman empire and the Russian area. This was an extension of the Mediterranean experience because the Greek language remained a fundamental component in the experience.

The basic experience of the Latin-speaking portion of the Roman empire also perdured until 1962. Indeed it was only in the last decade that the whole debate over the use of Latin was resolved. Up to then the culture and language traditions of the Mediterranean basin were the only ones given due consideration. We did not realize that every culture and language is sacred when it is part of the life of a consecrated Christian, whether that Christian is European, Papuan, or whatever. To be more precise, it is the consecrated Christian who gives sacredness to what he touches, speaks, and produces. All languages are sacred insofar as their speakers are consecrated people.

The *third* period has just begun. We might call it the period of crisis engendered by Vatican II. At this point someone might well complain about such a division of Church history, asserting that there were certainly many more periods and phases. But I would still maintain that a very good case can be made for the division I have presented here. I would say that we have only just moved beyond the second period of Church history outlined above. The evangelization of the Roman world and its perimeters—including Latin America—has been going on since 50 A.D. The tacit understanding was that the Church was meant only for Mediterranean peoples. Only with the advent of Vatican II have we come to realize pointedly that the Church was meant to be for the whole world. Only now have we begun to truly open up to the world outside the Mediterranean.

It will take more than a day to effect such openness. We will have to shed much cultural baggage in order to go out to the world at large. We are just beginning to realize, for example, that the Islamic world was never missionized. It was not interested in Latin, Greek, or the structures of the Roman and Byzantine world. Its experience was different, and it would have to be missionized from within the context of its own life. The Greco-Roman experience of the Mediterranean world did not leave much room for the evangelization of the Islamic world.

Neither were we able to truly go out and evangelize the Hindu or Chinese world. The latter is a very instructive instance. Matteo Ricci made direct contact with the Chinese emperor in the sixteenth century. The emperor was somewhat disposed towards conversion, but Rome opposed the idea of a Chinese rite. Speaking Chinese and dressed as a mandarin, Ricci arrived at the court and presented two gifts: an icon of the Virgin and a map of the world which also depicted the overall organization of the heavens. The Chinese emperor was impressed with Ricci's wisdom and explanations. Ricci, in turn, wanted to modify the Christian rituals so that they would conform to cultural beliefs and practices in China. When Ricci brought his request to Rome, he was refused. Latin, you see, was a sacred language but Chinese was not. So Ricci's great missionary exploit ended in failure.

Before I consider Christianity in Latin America, I should like to close this chapter with some remarks on Church history during the second long period described above.

## CHRISTIAN PERSECUTION IN THE ROMAN EMPIRE

There are two main phases in the second great period of Church history which I have outlined above. The first is the era of persecution, and it runs from about 50 A.D. to 313–314 A.D. During this phase Christians stood outside the established order, and the martyrs fearlessly faced that fact.

The martyrs were killed in the arena as atheists. We may feel that the Romans were ignorant indeed to kill Christians on such grounds. But if we are to appreciate the why and wherefore of their martyrdom, we must realize that they were "atheists" with respect to the Roman gods, and with respect to the values propounded by Roman culture. Such "atheism" is a serious matter indeed. To say that the sun was not a god was to empty temples all over the empire and to leave countless people without any gods. To say that the moon was not a goddess was to leave the night without any trace of divinity; and since the moon goddess was closely related to the earth goddess, it presaged catastrophic happenings in agriculture and field work. Finally, to say that the emperor was not a god was to engage in political subversion.

When we hear the early apologists saying that the moon and sun are not gods, we are likely to feel that their remarks are rather purposeless for us today. We forget that the "gods" change, and that we must always know who and what they are at a given moment. When the Christian does perform his prophetic task, when he points out that money or the existing political order is not a god, then his remarks take on a subversive tone and he is once more dragged into the arena. It is there that the enemies of the reigning false gods are taken care of. The true Christian will always have to die the death of a martyr, giving up his life for the sake of the Other. And the Other is the poor and lowly person who, like Jesus, does not have his own army. The martyr bears witness to the poor, for the sin of domination is fundamentally a denial of Jesus and God himself.

Consider all the theological revisions we are going to have to make. The death of the Christian martyrs in the Roman empire is something very relevant today because we have just started to get beyond the Mediterranean experience and we are feeling the full force of the rough weather ahead. This does not mean we should go back to the primitive Church of the first century. It does mean we are going to have to experience the full process of universalizing the Church which started then, and that certain features of the primitive Church are pertinent for us today.

Let us consider some of the features of the primitive Christian communities before Christianity became an established religion and turned into Christendom. First of all, there was a great deal of freedom in the area of liturgical innovation and inventiveness. Each community had its own liturgy. There was no "folk religion" because the devotion of the average person found expression in the key liturgical rites. Christian groups and grass-roots communities met to formulate their liturgies on the basis of simple frameworks which took their day-to-day life into account.

Second, these grass-roots communities were relatively small. People knew each other personally, so they could share each other's joys and sufferings. They were not the impersonal crowds that would come on the scene later.

Third, on the philosophical or theological level, there was a confrontation between two different ways of comprehending being and existence. The Indo-European outlook saw reality as that which was *present* and *permanent* before people's eyes. That was "being" (Greek *ousia*), and it was One. Hence in this view there was a strong thrust towards pantheism. Over against it stood Judaeo-Christian thought. Note that I say "Judaeo" because the first Christians were Jews for the most part, and because on the metaphysical level Christians did not contribute any new thesis. The vision of man and history held by the first Christians was a Jewish one. Christianity rooted this vision in Jesus Christ and thus formulated a new anthropological phase within Jewish tradition, but it did not introduce any metaphysical novelty.

What ensued was really "culture shock," perhaps the most interesting and noteworthy shock in world history. The Mediterranean community lived out this basic experience from *within* hellenistic culture. It had to transcend the existing horizon of Indo-European thought and inject a new horizon for understanding and comprehending existence. In so doing, it radically transformed the prevailing outlook, because the Greek world saw the being of the cosmos as something that was eternal and divine. Since Judaeo-Christian thought saw the cosmos as something created, it radically transformed everything. Christians desacralized the cosmos and its realities, making them tools of man. And this secularized cosmos is the modern world in which we now live. Man would never have reached the moon if that theological revolution had not occurred previously. It was a fundamental revolution in human history, and it was brought about by those early Christians who were persecuted in the first centuries of Church history.

Those early centuries are thus of the utmost importance. We will have to go back and study them more closely because we may presently find ourselves in a very similar situation. The situation of the Christian thinker today may be very similar to that of Justin, Tatian, and the other Christian apologists.

## CHRISTENDOM AS A SYSTEM

As time went on, Christianity turned into a political force. Thanks to Constantine, the Church persecuted became the Church triumphant. Constantine liberated the Church, possibly for political reasons. As a result the Church came to constitute what is referred to in theology as *Christendom*. The distinction between Christianity and Christendom is an important one. "Christianity" is the Christian religion. "Christendom" is a cultural reality. The former is a religion, the latter is a cultural totality which derives its basic orientation from Christianity. That is the way in which I am using the terms here.

Christendom first unified the liturgy and established it in a fixed form. Instead of continuing to grow and change with real life, the liturgy was fixed once and for all. Fluctuation and diversity could not be allowed much room in the new empire, so the number of differing liturgical families was gradually reduced. This process affected the Latin rite almost from the very start. In a relatively short time the Roman rite liturgy was, practically speaking, the only one left in the West. Simultaneously we see the appearance of huge conglomerates of people and of basilicas. In many cases these crowds of people were baptized and entrusted with a serious responsibility towards history without being adequately instructed. Unlike the early converts, these people were often baptized as children and hence entered the Church as such.

Some Christians realized that all this was quite remote from the Gospel message. They began to remove themselves to deserted areas, and even deserts. As the Church became the majority force, monasticism also began to come into prominence. Men and women devoted to God began to realize that their culture was not Christian. The fact is that no culture as such can be Christian, because Christianity can never be a culture. Those who are "gathered together" by Christ form a Church, not a culture. Christendom, as a cultural totality, was a mixture of Christian and hellenistic elements. It was a political unity. Hence Constantine convened and dissolved Councils. Theological disputes were often bound up with other issues, including economic ones. The course of a Council might be affected by such questions as whether the crops of Alexandria could be sold in Constantinople.

Christendom was not just an ecclesiastical unity; it was also a military and economic unity. The bishops who had lived under persecution now became important authorities, passing judgment on a variety of issues. Ambrose, for example, forced an emperor to get down on his knees before him. Simultaneously this culture, now labelled "Christian," became a matter of tradition. What it meant to be a Christian was taken as something well known and obvious, and it was handed down from generation to generation. One became a Christian by birth, not by *conversion*, and people stopped asking what it really meant to be a Christian.

This mixture of Christianity and culture known as Christendom had its own philosophy. It was predominantly Platonic or Neoplatonic in cast, although its panoply of logic was more or less Aristotelian. The great Fathers of the Church around this time—Origen, Irenaeus, Basil, Gregory, and Augustine—were well versed in philosophy. All of them were faced with problems that could not be solved in terms of hellenistic conceptualization. Origen's book on first principles, is a model example of their problems and procedures.

In this book Origen tries to be a hellenist for the hellenists and a Christian for the Christians. His anthropological doctrine goes something like this. In the beginning God created pure spirits. Some sinned excessively; they were the demons. Some sinned slightly; they were the angels. Others sinned moderately. For them God created the material cosmos and inserted them into bodies; they are the souls of human beings. On the one hand Origen wants to defend the doctrine of creation; on the other hand he wants to uphold the body-soul dualism. For him, man is an unstable unity of soul and imprisoning body. When man dies, his immortal soul will be set free whereas his mortal body will suffer corruption and decay. This much is acceptable to the Greek. To satisfy the Christian, however, he must also include the whole aspect of resurrection. Origen seems to do this insofar as he does maintain that the body will rise again. But the fact is that his risen body is so spiritualized that it is really a pure and unsullied soul.

Now it might seem that Origen did succeed in defending both a Christian and a Greek doctrine. But the fact is that Christianity has never taught "the resurrection of *the body.*" It talks about the "resurrection of the dead" or the resurrection "of the flesh." The dangers inherent in Origen's thought were soon sensed, and opposition to him grew. This critical conflict, which deserves our attention, was centered in Alexandria because that city was a focus of culture and of hellenism. The "school of Alexandria," which began with Clement, taught a doctrine of "gnosis." It was a Christian "gnosis," to be sure, and it continued to grow as time went on. Gradually this hellenizing theology sought to work out an epistemological approach which would bring it in line with the approach of Aristotle. In this form it came to the West, and theology lost all sense of history and its meaning.

A new start was made in the nineteenth century by the Tübingen School. Hegel, Schelling, and Hölderlin studied in the Lutheran school of theology in Tübingen, and Hegel's thought would have a profound influence on Ferdinand Baur. A few blocks away, Möhler was teaching at the Catholic seminary. One might well say that modern theology stems from the basic notion of "salvation history" (*Heilsgeschichte*), which enabled theology to recover its sense of history after centuries of neglect.

## BYZANTINE, LATIN,
## AND HISPANIC CHRISTENDOM

In the fourth century A.D., there were distinct geo-cultural spheres in Christendom. Byzantine Christendom had its focal point in the city of Constantinople, the chief city of Christendom. Constantinople came into being as a Christian city and faded out as a Christian city—struggling to the very end to preserve Christian culture as a unity. Constantine founded it in 330 A.D. with the aim of making it the seat of a new empire, allying himself to the Christian majority living in Anatolia. As a seat of Christian culture it met its demise in 1453, when it was conquered by the Turks. It was the only center of Christian culture, the only version of Christendom, which went through its full cycle.

From Byzantine Christendom there arose the Russian version of Christendom. The Russians, who appeared on the scene for the first time in the ninth century, derived from the Varangians. The latter were Scandinavian traders and warriors (the word *Wahr* signifies "economic goods" or "merchandise"). The Russians came into contact with Byzantium and eventually built the third Rome: Moscow. This Russian culture was a marginal Byzantine culture. Through it, Christendom moved eastward and reached the Pacific Ocean.

Latin Christendom was much smaller in numbers at the start of the fourth century. Due to the civilizing efforts of the monks, the newly arrived Germanic tribes were evangelized and the foundations of a future Europe were laid. It would be a Europe dominated by Christendom, thanks to the baptism of various barbarian leaders.

Soon Spain boasted great theologians and saints. Isidore of Seville was the last representative of the tradition embodied in the Latin Church Fathers. In 710–711 A.D., this tradition was buried under the encroaching wave of Arab invaders. From 718 A.D. on, the effort to expel these invaders gave shape and form to Spain. By the sixteenth century the Christian people of Spain were inured to war. The ideals of Christendom and Crusade continued to live on in Spain long after they had faded from the consciousness of other peoples in Europe, because the struggle against the Muslims continued for many centuries. They gradually pushed back the frontiers of the encroaching Muslims, conquering Granada in the same year that Columbus discovered America.

These frontier-fighters continued their struggle here in the new world, crusading against the native empires of this region. Only when victory was achieved here did these warriors lay down their arms. It was all part of one great battle, which extended over almost a thousand years. If one does not realize that fact, one cannot understand the events which took place here from 1492 on. It is the old ideal of the Christian cavalier that is upheld by Cortez, Pizarro, and the other conquistadores. It is Latin Christendom, in its hispanic form, that is brought to our shores.

## NOTES

1. Mircea Eliade, *Patterns in Comparative Religion,* Eng. Trans. (New York: Sheed & Ward, 1958), pp. 345–56.

2. See my book *El humanismo helénico* (Buenos Aires: Eudeba, 1975).

3. See my book *El humanismo semita* (Buenos Aires: Eudeba, 1969).

4. Paul Ricoeur, *The Symbolism of Evil,* Eng. Trans. (New York: Harper & Row, 1967). See Part II, Chapter 3, for example.

5. Paul Ricoeur, *Freud and Philosophy: An Essay on Interpretation,* Eng. Trans. (New Haven: Yale University Press, 1970).

6. For some interesting remarks on man's dread of history, faith, and the unforeseen, see the last chapter of Eliade's book, *Myth of the Eternal Return: Cosmos and History* (Princeton University Press, 1954).

# 3

# Colonial Christendom
# in Latin America

Now we come to our own version of Christian culture. For
our purposes here we may consider it still another version
of Christendom. It is the "Christendom of the Indies" of
which Toribio de Mogrovejo spoke in his letters around the
start of the Third Council of Lima in 1582–83. And our
version of Christendom, unlike that of the Byzantine empire and that of the Roman empire, has been a colonial one.
We have been on the periphery, while the previous versions of Christendom have been in the center.

## THE ONLY COLONIAL VERSION
## OF CHRISTENDOM

It is important for us to realize that our version of Christendom is the only _colonial_ or dependent version. To discover
in what sense it is "colonial" is to discover—theologically,
philosophically, and historically—who we are as Latin
American Christians. To cease being "colonial" is to liberate
ourselves and become part of the larger world—without
imposing on the rest of the world the oppressive bonds of a
single culture. In my opinion this has become possible only
since Vatican II. We are now in a position to get beyond the

75

limits of Mediterranean culture and to truly evangelize the world of Africa and Asia.

Almost against its will, Christianity is being stripped of its cultural baggage. Leaving "Christendom" behind, it is beginning to get back its freedom. To some people this process of secularization seems to spell decline and disaster. But in all likelihood the Old Testament prophets would explain it as a punishment for sin and a process of

THRUST OF CONQUEST
NAVIGATION ROUTES
EXTENT OF CONQUEST

THE SEQUENCE OF
SPANISH AND PORTUGUESE
CONQUEST

liberation—which is how they described Israel's exile in Babylon. The secularist persecution of the Church in the seventeenth, eighteenth, and nineteenth centuries may have reduced the Church to dire poverty. But that very poverty will now free the Church to truly preach the Gospel message. Once again the hand of the unbeliever has been

God's instrument for liberating his Church so that it might carry out its true mission. As we shall note along the way, the process of expropriation has not been confined to property and possessions. It has also affected pastoral attitudes and the theological and exegetical structures of the Church.

Let us begin back in 1492 when Columbus arrived here just about the same time that the Catholic rulers of Spain were recapturing their country from the Moslems. Columbus set foot on the most primitive part of America, landing in the Caribbean region. It was the most primitive part of America in the sense that the Indians there were planters living in a paleolithic setting. They had no great urban civilization, and the initial impact of European conquest would be decisive.

When the lookout shouted "Land ho!" Columbus already had a name picked out for this land—even before he set foot on it. He called it San Salvador. Our destiny was decided for us from the very beginning. Columbus did not come on land and ask the inhabitants: "Who are you? What is the name of this place?" He gave it a name. In the biblical understanding of this process, to give someone or something a name is to gain dominion over what is named. So our destiny was taken in hand with the first voyage of discovery.

Columbus also placed the natives under the charge of his own people, commending them to his regal patrons. The *encomienda* system began right then and there, although it would take time for it to be organized and legislated.

One might well say that Amerindia, the mother of Latin America, has been oppressed since the very start of Europe's arrival on the scene. The American Indian, the Other, was subjugated right at the beginning. It is a very important point and has very concrete manifestations. We must remember that it was Spanish men who came to America, and that they came alone. It was the Indian women of America who served as their concubines, giving birth to the *mestizo,* who is the true Latin American. Yet little or nothing has been written about the Indian mother of America. She is one of the oppressed mothers of history, and she has been such for a very long time. It was she who had to endure the potency of the oppressive conqueror from Europe. Nietzsche spoke about the "will to power," but he had nothing to say about the other side of the coin. Over against the reality of the "will to power" stands the reality of the "oppressed will." We can see the latter reality very well because we can look at past, present, and future from the vantage point of the poor and the oppressed.

Spain's experience with Christianity was wholly an experience with Christendom. Great reformer that he was, Archbishop Jiménez de Cisneros (1436–1517) also possessed palaces and armies. The king had to deal with the Archbishop in order to enact his own plans. Thanks to Rome's weakness, on the other hand, the king had the right to nominate bishops and his nominations usually were accepted. Thus the king of Spain chose all our bishops during the colonial period. Moreover, the Latin American Church was governed by the Council of the Indies from 1524 on. This Council had charge of everything in America, and it passed laws on a wide variety of matters. It decided whether some enterprise would be initiated, whether a war would be undertaken, whether a diocese would be founded, whether missionaries would be sent, and so forth.

In many instances the head or director of the Council of the Indies was a bishop, but laymen actually did the work of administration. That was Christendom: a culture of which Christianity was a "part." And thus the equivocal nature of the whole arrangement, for the Church was one element in a cultural whole. It had to serve other ends, rendering obedience to the State and serving it in different ways. Bishops would report on the activities of viceroys, and viceroys would report on the activities of bishops. The bishop had economic power because he collected tithes. This income was then taken over by the king, but he shared it amply. The bishop also had political influence because he had great authority in the eyes of the people. On the other side of the coin, however, the viceroy exercised spiritual faculties. He could decide where a cathedral would be located, and he sometimes had the right to jail ecclesiastics who had violated laws. Disputes and conflicts broke out repeatedly between the two sides. The king operated on a policy of divide and conquer.

In any case a new culture came into being. The important point I want to bring out here is that Christianity is a Church which transcends every culture. Christendom, on the other hand, was a culture which subsumed Christianity as one of its elements. Insofar as Christianity did not conform to its cultural requirements, however, it was attacked by the totality that was Christendom. Thus the Jesuits were expelled from America in 1767, because they were the only religious order which would not allow the king to have charge of the sending of missionaries. In the eyes of the king, the Jesuits were a fifth column, because they challenged the power of his administrative organs. In addition, the Jesuit missions here were really States within the State, and regal absolutism could not tolerate that. When the Church chose to act autonomously, it suffered expulsion and persecution. When it did not choose to act that way, it became one more element in a cultural totality and thereby abdicated the Christian function of prophetic criticism.

Latin American Christendom had different periods too. The first period, from 1492 to 1808, was one of great expansion in the life of this colonial Christendom. The appearance of independence movements in 1808 heralded the start of a period of crisis for this culture, and the crisis continued right down to 1962. All of us have felt the impact of this crisis to some extent in our day-to-day lives. In fact I would say that our spiritual and theological crisis stems from the fact that we have had to live through two different ecclesial experiences at the same time. A third period began for us, and for the Church around the world, in 1962. It is the period through which we are now living, and I will discuss it in some detail in the next chapter.

If we want to understand what is happening today, we must understand what happened in the nineteenth century. But we must also understand what happened before that. In an earlier book of mine (*Hipótesis para una historia de la Iglesia en América latina*) I noted certain trends in the number of religious in Chile over a period of time. In 1700 there were eight religious per 10,000 people; in 1800 there were ten religious per 10,000 people; in 1960—and the figures are now more exact—there was one religious per 10,000 inhabitants. That suggests what has happened to the Church in the course of time, and we must look at the situation with open eyes if we want to adopt the right pastoral approach. The considerable presence of the Church in an earlier day has diminished considerably, and we must make pastoral decisions on the basis of that fact.

Near Nazareth there is a small town called Cana. One afternoon, during my two years in Israel as a laborer, I met an old Orthodox priest in Cana. The bearded old man of seventy talked to me about his family. He had eight children, now grown, and many grandchildren. I asked him how he happened to become a priest, and he told me. When he was forty years old, he already had eight children and was working his land. The priest of Cana died, and the Christians of the town got together to choose a new priest. They chose him. He then spent six months in Jerusalem where he went back to studying the liturgy which he had learned in childhood. Once he had refreshed his memory on the details, he came back as a priest to the people of his town. This married man is part of *the oldest tradition* of the Church. The practice is not something new; it has been going on since the beginning. There is nothing new about suggesting that married men be ordained priests, as a look at history will indicate. It is our oldest tradition, still carried on by the Byzantine Orthodox and the Catholic Melchites.

My point is that there was a large number of priestly vocations in Latin Christendom and the Spanish Church. Hence it was possible to impose stipulations which would cut down the number of candidates and which in effect turned priests into monks. Even with these stipulations, the number of priests was large. But our situation is very different today. Both theology and history offer us valid grounds for re-examining the whole question and going back to the older tradition of the Church. We no longer live in the age of Christendom. Our situation today is quite different.

This suggests that our solutions might also differ very much from those of Europe. In France, for example, there are 45,000 priests. In all of Latin America there are only 30,000 priests. But Latin America is twenty times larger than France. So we must deal with our real situation in history as it is, not as others deal with their different situation. The number of priests and consecrated religious in Latin America is now infinitesimal. The whole question must be reconsidered from top to bottom.

## THE FIRST PROPHETS IN LATIN AMERICA

Before I discuss the various periods of Church history in Latin America. I should like to mention several important figures in our early Church history. We too have had our prophets, and the first great figure in that tradition was the Dominican Antonio de Montesinos. On the third Sunday of Advent in 1511 he cited the prophetic texts of Isaiah and John the Baptist to launch an attack on the way the native Indians were being treated by the Spaniards in the *encomiendas*. The Spaniards' behavior was a mortal sin, he said, and he would not give them absolution henceforth.

Montesinos thereby proclaimed that there was a real difference between Christianity and hispanic culture. He interpreted present history and gave it *meaning* in the light of the
biblical texts. Prophetic re-reading of the Gospel led him to
prophetic action. He realized that he, as a man of the
Church, was not simply a tool of Spanish culture; he was
something more. He took this position, and it would be
defended and upheld by Pedro de Córdoba and the
brothers of the monastery of Hispaniola. It would also be
the banner carried by another great figure: Bartolomé de
Las Casas.

We do not really know when Bartolomé de Las Casas was
ordained a priest. He had come to the New World in 1502
with his father and was later ordained. At first he was just
another priest who had Indians working for him. His real
conversion began in 1514, after he had heard something of
the preaching of Montesinos and read the biblical denunci-
ation of injustice. Thanks to the charism of prophecy, he
was able to see that his style of life entailed a contradiction.
So he began a mission that would last until his death in
1566.

First he went to talk with Montesinos, then he headed for
Spain. He made contact with Jiménez de Cisneros, and
ultimately the latter was persuaded to designate him as the
"Universal Protector of the Indians of the Indies."[1] Thus a
clear distinction was finally made between Spanish culture
and the missionary role of the Church, even though it
would usually not be observed in practice or accepted by
most people. Actually few missionaries took cognizance of
the difference between being Spanish and being a Christian, although some did complain about the anti-
evangelical impact of the forced amalgam. One bishop, for
example, reported the raids of Spanish conquistadores into
Indian settlements. He described to the king how they
robbed the Indians and killed their women and children in
New Spain and New Granada. This, he said, caused the

Indians to flee to the mountains and to identify Christianity with Spanish cruelty.

But for the most part the Church itself identified its life with that of Spanish civilization and its culture. This is the attitude which pervaded the colonial period and dramatically marked its life. When we talk about the separation of Church and State today, we can hear the echoes of our past history in the debate that rages. In my opinion we will be much better off when we finally manage to make a clear distinction between Spanish culture and Christianity—as Bartolomé de Las Casas did several centuries ago.

Las Casas prophetically espoused a new task: nonviolent evangelization. He wanted the Indians to be converted by the force of the Gospel message, not by force of arms. This is the course he proposed for the evangelization of Cumaná, in present-day northeast Venezuela. His project failed because the situation was already bad there. Certain Spaniards had been exploiting and killing the Indians before he arrived. Subsequently, however, Bishop Francisco Marroquín of Guatemala invited him to evangelize the Indians in his territory. Las Casas succeeded in converting the Indians with his peaceful approach, and his experience helped to lead up to the promulgation of the *New Laws* in 1542.

The point to be noted here is that Spanish "messianism" identified Christianity with Spanish culture. When the Church accepted this identification, it encountered great difficulties in carrying out its redemptive work. When the Church managed to separate itself and its work from Spanish culture, on the other hand, the Gospel message made great headway among the Indians. The Reductions are a case in point. The first to entertain the notion of Reductions was Vasco de Quiroga, who eventually became the bishop of the Tarascan Indians in Michoacán, Mexico. Vasco de Quiroga was a layman for most of his life. An official of the Mexican *audiencia*, he settled down among the

Indians after he had reached the age of sixty. He was a humanist who had been greatly impressed by his reading of Thomas More's works, of his *Utopia* in particular. He therefore decided to set up Christian societies outside the sphere of direct Spanish contact. He was a great civilizer and missionary, who was ultimately designated as a bishop by the king.

Vasco de Quiroga regarded himself as bishop to the Indians, not to the Spaniards. He never managed to get a cathedral built because he spent his whole time with the Indians. Under his direction, over 150 Indian villages were set up for the Tarascans. They were admirably organized, and thus the first contact of these Indians with Spanish influence was a relatively happy one. This was the start of the diocese of Michoacán.

There were many other men of the caliber of Vasco de Quiroga, and we shall mention some of them as we proceed. Right now, however, I want to briefly discuss the various stages of Church history in Latin America.

## THE FIRST STEPS (1492–1519)

I think it is most interesting and worthwhile to explore the distinct features and stages of our Church history, and I have done that to some extent in my book cited earlier.[2] But it is also worthwhile for us to consider the overall course of that history briefly here.

Church history began in Latin America with the arrival of the first evangelizers, and that took place in the Caribbean region. Hence it occurred among very primitive Indians. We must realize that it is impossible to teach history without adverting to social typology to some extent. One must know what kind of Indians were involved and whether they were really in a position to accept Christianity.

The Caribbean Indians encountered by Columbus and his crew were among the most primitive in Amerindia.

They included such groups as the Caribs, the Arawaks, and the Tupis, who had descended through Florida and spread out over the Caribbean. Some had gone farther, occupying the northern and central parts of Brazil. Using small canoes and ingenious navigation instruments, they moved about from island to island. Their standard of living was extremely low. They were vegetarians. Since it was difficult to feed young children, mothers nursed their young until the age of five or six years. As a result, there was a low birth rate. When the Spaniards arrived, these fragile people were stricken with the diseases imported from Europe: tuberculosis, syphilis, and so forth. The Indians were quickly decimated and the Spaniards did not meet with much physical resistance.

A great problem was the great diversity of languages and the absence of any political organization. There were no republics or kingdoms or empires in this immediate area, just a conglomeration of tribes or clans. The task of evangelizing was thus rendered impossible, and the first impression held of the Indians was a very negative one. The Indians either died or were forced into the *encomiendas*. If that had been all there was to America, then Spain would have done nothing and America would not have been born. The unfortunate thing, however, is that mistakes were made during this first period. The Indians died from diseases and ill treatment. This whole side of the picture is reflected by Bartolomé de Las Casas in the *Destruction of the Indies*, where he describes the disappearance of Indian culture in the face of Spanish incursion.

The Spanish could not evangelize this culture because its extremely low level did not allow for dialogue. We are dealing with a completely negative period, which lasted until around 1517–1519. It was then that Diego Velázquez, the governor of Cuba, conceived the idea of organizing the conquest of the region that had recently been discovered.

## THE EVANGELIZATION OF MEXICO
## AND PERU (1519–1551)

Up to 1519 no great culture had been encountered in the course of Spanish exploration and conquest. This first epoch, however, was a decisive one and deserves to be studied very closely. For it was during this earliest period that the first form of many institutions took shape: the *encomiendas,* the *cabildos,* and the first outlines of the *audiencias.* The Church began to resign itself to the defects of the conquest, but it also began to voice its first prophetic denunciations.

A new and different epoch began in 1519. A lieutenant of Velázquez rose up in revolt. Daring as he was, the lieutenant then launched the conquest of the Yucatan. Thus Hernando Cortez happened upon the existence of an empire, and word began to spread about a mature and important civilization that was fabulously wealthy.

This would change the whole course of evangelization, because the newly discovered peoples had a solid culture of a much higher sort. The Spaniards were able to conquer much more in a short period of time, taking advantage of the structures which these peoples already possessed. The Spaniards conquered Mexico and set themselves up in the capital. Evangelization *en masse* began with the arrival of the so-called "Twelve Apostles" in 1524. They were the extraordinary Franciscans who set out through Mexican territory to convert the people to Christianity.

Today we can appreciate the caliber of those missionaries. They came from sixteenth-century Spain, the Spain in which John of the Cross and Saint Teresa flourished, the Spain which was flooded with noble ideals of holiness and gentlemanly knighthood. One of these missionaries was Motolinía (Toribio de Benavente). Barefoot, he traversed all of Mexico. The Indians called him "the poor one" because he was even poorer than they. He

88     HISTORY AND THE THEOLOGY OF LIBERATION

learned the Aztec language quickly and preached fluently in that language. Indeed all those early missionaries learned the native idiom so well that other Spaniards complained about the fact that the Indians were not learning Spanish. They felt that the policy of the Church was hindering the spread of Spanish.

For some time it was the Church that held up the spread of Spanish culture and language in America. And it did so for the sake of its missionary endeavors. But millions of people were now involved, and some sort of political organization was necessary. It must be remembered, however, that only Castile was involved in the thrust towards America. Aragon was deeply enmeshed in European politics. Up until 1519 America was insignificant and did not produce a red cent.

The age of splendor began in 1519, and it was then that the first great ecclesiastics arrived on the scene. In 1528 Juan de Zumárraga arrived and salvaged Mexico from the disastrous first *audiencia*. Bishop Julián Garcés, a Dominican, arrived in the area of Tlaxcala. Vasco de Quiroga came to Michoacán and Marroquín to Guatemala. Many other fine bishops arrived on the scene, along with secular priests and thousands of missionary Dominicans, Franciscans, and Mercedarians. Much later the Jesuits would come also. Gradually the Church began to organize here. Florida was made a bishopric in 1520, Mexico City in 1530. Other bishoprics were gradually established, centered around Santo Domingo. This was the focal point in the first period, but gradually Mexico City gained preeminence.

Subsequently Pizarro discovered Peru. He was greatly supported by García Díaz Arias, who would become the first bishop of Quito. It was Arias who contributed much of the money for Pizarro's enterprise, encouraged him in spirit, and gave purpose to the undertaking. Once the Spanish had conquered those two great American empires, the situation was greatly changed. Now America had a solidity of its own. Then the region of the Chibchas was discovered as the two exploring parties, one coming from the north and the other from the south, met somewhere in between. New Granada came into being with the help of Sebastián de Benalcázar and his companions. Other bishoprics sprang up also: Santa Fe de Bogotá, Santa María, and Coro; Panamá in Central America. In short order there were twenty-five dioceses with the organizational structure required for their maintenance.

## THE ORGANIZATION OF THE CHURCH (1551–1620)

A new stage began in 1551. The first great attempt at evangelizing America had come to a close, although the primitive areas of Brazil and Argentina had not yet been touched. The Spanish element certainly did not disregard the Amerindian element. Instead it planted its root in what was already in existence. And there was good reason for going by way of the Pacific coast. It would have been much easier to move up along the southern Atlantic coast towards the Río de la Plata on southeast South America. But the Indians in that whole region were a wretched lot with an impoverished prehistory. The region with a great prehistory was centered on the Pacific coast, and it is there that the Church was set up in all its splendor.

The colonial Church had two great centers. One was Mexico City, the capital of the Aztec empire. The other was Lima, situated in the heart of the Inca empire. It is there that the Church established its great universities and its printing presses; from there its influence and life spread throughout the newly discovered region. In other words, the two most important archepiscopal sees were established on the sites of the two great American empires. The foundations of the Church in America were not artificial creations.

The interesting thing, of course, is that the areas on the

Atlantic coast would eventually prove to be the most prosperous ones. While Pizarro conquered the flourishing Inca empire at one fell swoop, the southern *pampas* would be conquered only slowly during the course of the nineteenth century. Yet the latter region is a richer one today.

Thoroughgoing organization of the newly established American Church began in 1551. The first provincial Council of Lima took place in that year. It was under the directorship of Jerónimo de Loaisa, who served as bishop and then archbishop for several decades. His function was a major one, and he received and dealt with many viceroys. Loaisa, in fact, is the great figure in Peru during this period. He is much more significant than Diego de Almagro and Pizarro, for example. After him will come Toribio de Mogrovejo, a truly imposing figure, who was the leading spirit in Peru from 1580 to 1606 even though the viceroy of the time, Francisco de Toledo, was also an outstanding man.

As I mentioned, the first provincial Council of Lima was held in 1551. These provincial councils are important in our history and deserve close study. The first meeting of this kind, as far as I can tell from my study in various archives, was the Synod of Guatemala in 1536. As far as I can reconstruct this matter, there were about seventy-two diocesan synods between 1536 and 1636. They were truly autochthonous in nature. They dealt almost exclusively with the evangelization of the Indians, with the languages involved, and with the needs and demands imposed on priests and catechists. In other words, it was in no way an "imported" Church. It was a Church making great efforts to face up to the real situation. The complexity of that situation surpassed its capabilities, but the Church worked harder and more earnestly then to face the situation than it ever has since—in my opinion.

The sixteenth century was a golden age, and the year 1551 was a momentous date for the Church. Loaisa set forth eighteen ordinances for his missionaries. In very concrete terms these ordinances spelled out how they were to carry out their mission and what behavior was incumbent on one who sought to be an authentic missionary. Such was the realistic outlook of the bishops in this period as one council or synod succeeded another. There were two councils in Mexico and a second in Peru. Then came the third Council of Lima, which is now considered the great Church council of the colonial epoch. It was convened by Toribio de Mogrovejo, and we must consider him and his accomplishments.

Toribio was a young layman presiding over the Inquisition of Granada, and he had a deep acquaintance with the recently converted Moslems. He had been well educated at Salamanca, and he even entertained ideas about being a professor there. He had just been tonsured when Philip proposed that he succeed Loaisa in Lima. At the age of forty-two Toribio accepted the proposal, left his native country behind, and set out for the wilds of Peru. As soon as he arrived in Lima, he made contact with the Indians and began regular rounds of visitation that would carry him throughout the region. His trips would last five years; they say he covered 40,000 miles on foot, visiting many places where no Spaniard had been before. Besides these regular visitations, he convened twelve diocesan synods and three provincial Church councils. Toribio is one of the great holy men of America, a bishop who embodied the true missionary ideal. The Indians loved him like a father, regarding him almost like a divine Inca because of his total commitment and his absolute poverty. He hardly ever lived in his episcopal palace because of his long visitations, and he had nothing of his own to leave behind when he died.[3]

In my opinion, this period of Church history ends either with the death of Toribio de Mogrovejo in 1606 or else in 1620, because it is at about that time that the last large dioceses are set up—Durango in the north and Buenos Aires in the south. Missionary work will continue to some extent, a few lesser dioceses will come into being later, but by 1620 the ecclesiastical organization of America was practically complete.

This was the third period in Latin American Church history as I see it. Missionary work had converted the vast mass of Indians who had been brought into contact with the Spanish, and various diocesan synods and regional councils had been held. But you may ask: To what extent had the Indians really been evangelized? There is no reason to minimize or make fun of this evangelization *en masse*. It is true that in many areas it was quite superficial, that it was not authentic evangelization at all. But as Robert Ricard points out in his book *The Spiritual Conquest of Mexico* (Eng. trans., Berkeley: University of California Press, 1966), the areas that were well evangelized in the sixteenth century are those which have remained Christian, at least in name, right up to today—even though it is what we would call a folk Catholicism. The regions that were poorly evangelized, on the other hand, are the very regions that have been impregnated with paganism and other influences alien to Christianity. So one might well say that the early missionary work was not as superficial as it might seem, and that it had enormous effectiveness. In any case this era came to an end somewhere in the first part of the seventeenth century. One might date its close in 1620; or in 1623, with the death of Philip III; or in 1625, with the celebration of the first Council of Santa Fe de Bogotá; or in 1629, with the celebration of the first Council of La Plata de los Charcas, which was convened by Bishop Hernando Arias de Ugarte.

This bishop deserves a word too. He was an extraordinary man, who had been a member of the *audiencia* of Panamá. He served successively as Bishop of Quito, Archbishop of Santa Fe de Bogotá, Archbishop of La Plata de los Charcas, and Archbishop of Lima. He was of the same temper as Toribio de Mogrovejo. He travelled through the countryside of his people on the back of a mule, and

convened two great councils to confront the pastoral
problems imposed by the poverty and hard life of his
flock.

## THE SEVENTEENTH CENTURY
## IN HISPANO-AMERICA

A period of stabilization now began. It is the start of the
colonial period as we tend to envision it today. The boundaries between the native Indians and the immigrant
Spaniards began to harden. Missionaries stopped speaking
to the Indians in their native Indian tongues as royal de-
crees forced the Indians to learn Spanish. Those who had
been converted to Christianity in the sixteenth century
remained Christian. Those who had not yet been converted
to Christianity tended now to retreat to the isolated hill
country and forest. They would revert to paganism such as
we still encounter it today.

The seventeenth century is a distinctive period, marked
by conflicting factions. Arguments arose between diocesan
bishops and religious clergy, between the Jesuits and the
Dominicans. The Jesuits had a policy of their own, one
which I would say was somewhat separatist. It can be seen
clearly in the establishment of the University of Lima. The
Dominicans had set up a university in their monastery.
Bishop Loaisa wanted to convert it into a great diocesan
university in which all the religious orders would be involved, but the Jesuits refused to participate in the scheme.
Eventually the university was set up as Loaisa had
wanted—outside the Dominican monastery—but the
Jesuits would not get involved in it. The Jesuits organized
their extraordinary projects in many different areas, but
they always stood apart from everyone else to some extent.

The bitter conflicts of this period help to explain why the
Jesuits were eventually expelled. They took a strong stand
for their own independence vis-à-vis the crown, a stand

which we today would regard as positive. It was the only religious order that was not under the control of the crown. Thanks to papal concessions, it was the king who set up missionary groups, provided for their training in Seville, and then sent them to America. In a sense they were envoys of the king. The Franciscans and Dominicans were under the authority of the Council of the Indies. The Jesuits never accepted this arrangement. They took their orders from their General in Rome. In the pervading atmosphere of exaggerated Spanish nationalism, the Jesuits represented an element of universalism and unwanted contact with Rome. The Spanish king could not accept this, although the attitude of the Jesuits was a laudable one in my opinion.

In America the Jesuits did not support the policies of the bishops. There was continuing conflict betweeen the bishops and the Jesuits, and among the various religious orders themselves. The reason for this is that in this period we see the start of a process which I shall call "secularization," although I do not mean it in the sense that we use the term today. Here I am referring to the fact that the Christian missions, originally set up by religious missionaries, began to be turned over to the secular (or diocesan) clergy. These settlements had been established by the hard work of missionary religious. Now many of these settlements were Christian and prosperous, bringing in wealth to the Church. The bishops felt that these settlements should now be turned over to the secular clergy, that the proper role of the missionary religious was to keep pushing back the frontiers of paganism, to be the "advance men" of the Christian religion. This position was not accepted, and it gave rise to many arguments and disputes.

We must remember that there was no shortage of clergy at that time. At one point Toribio de Mogrovejo noted that he had more priests than he knew what to do with. So there was more than enough clergy to go around, and even the

remotest areas were visited by priests. This was the situation
in the closing years of the sixteenth century and the early
days of the seventeenth century. In Lima, for example,
there were two language cathedras: one for Quechua and
one for Aymara. To be ordained to the priesthood, a candi-
date had to know one of the two languages in addition to his
theology. The Aymara cathedra was a very important one.
In those days priests evangelized the people in their own
language. Today many people in Peru still speak only their
native language, but they are no longer evangelized in their
native tongue.

Whether we like it or not, our history can be explained in
part on the basis of events in Spain. (I do not say this as a
Hispanophile.) The fact is that the sixteenth century was a
golden age for Spain, when it boasted a lofty culture and
held first place in Europe. All this came tumbling down in
the seventeenth century, and we too felt the impact of the
collapse.

## THE BOURBON DECADENCE (1700–1808)

From 1700 to 1808 we find ourselves in the era of the
Bourbons. America lost much of its importance and the
Church fossilized even more. It was a sad era, in the sense
that nothing radically new appeared on the scene. The only
positive note might be the fact that missionaries continued
to forge ahead in the north—first the Jesuits, then the
Franciscans after the former had been expelled.

The expulsion of the Jesuits took place in 1767 in Brazil,
1769 elsewhere. To say that it was an event of critical importance would probably be an understatement. More than
2200 Jesuits left America, and they had been the elite in the
universities and communities. It was they who had been
studying physics and chemistry and trying to formulate a
modern philosophy and theology. The places left vacant by

their expulsion were filled by Franciscans and Dominicans, but for the most part they could not fill the shoes of their predecessors. It was the first tremor of collapse in the system known as Christendom.

It is my belief that much that happened later, in the catastrophic nineteenth century for example, can be traced back to this blow. If the Jesuits had remained on the scene, things could very easily have taken a very different course. In Mendoza, for example, the Jesuits had operated a fine academy. Its closing left no educational institution of importance in Mendoza. Only after the movement for independence would we see the start of a National College sponsored by the State.

The missionary enterprise was continued throughout the eighteenth century. In the north of Mexico, for example, the Jesuits reached California as early as 1607. But not until the extraordinary Fray Junípero Serra (1713–1784) began his work was there missionary activity of the same calibre as "the early days." The Franciscans arrived in 1768 to replace the Jesuits. Working with amazing diligence, they established their mission outposts and *reducciones*. Starting at San Diego, founded by Fray Junípero in 1769, they reached San Francisco in 1776. The Dominicans as well founded reductions throughout Upper California.

## THE SOCIAL STRUGGLE
## AND THE MARTYR BISHOPS

Here I should like to mention a figure who stands out in my mind. The Christian, the saint, is a martyr. There is nothing better one can do than give one's life for the poor. Bishop Antonio de Valdivieso of Nicaragua, was undoubtedly a martyr in the colonial era. He was the Bishop of Central America, a contemporary of Bartolomé de Las Casas and several other great bishops. As the documents from that period will tell you, the Indians of that region were being exploited terribly. Valdivieso took his life in his hands by seeking to take the Indians out of the *encomiendas,* as the New Laws of 1542 permitted, and place them at the disposal of the king himself as free people. The governor of Nicaragua at that time, a man named Rodrigo de Contreras, eventually had the bishop assassinated for his insistent defense of the Indians. Valdivieso, who is scarcely remembered now at all, died a martyr's death in defense of the native population.

Between 1540 and 1560 there were more than twenty bishops who dedicated their lives to the defense of the Indians. Pablo de Torres, the bishop of Panamá, was expelled from his diocese for that reason. Juan del Valle, bishop of Popayán, strove mightily to defend the Indians in his region. When his efforts seemed to be of no avail, he went to appeal to the *audiencia* of Santa Fe de Bogotá. When that effort failed, he headed back to Europe to appeal to the Council of the Indies. And when that venture brought no results, he packed up his documents on mules and headed for the Council of Trent. He died somewhere in France on the way to the Council.

His story is a bit like the course of Church history here in Latin America. He tried to make contact directly with Rome, but he never succeeded. Rome never spoke directly with Latin America; she spoke to it through the Spanish king and the Council of the Indies. Rome had no immediate presence here. When our wars for independence came, the new leaders pleaded directly with Rome to accept our political independence. But Rome was deeply involved with the Austrian empire and France. She could not accept Latin American independence, and condemned it in 1816. There is actually an encyclical condemning our revolution, our struggle for independence. San Martín was not only regarded as a traitor by Spain; he was also condemned by the Pope.

COLONIAL CHRISTENDOM IN CRISIS (1808–1825)

With the rise of the movement for independence, the colonial Christendom that had existed since the arrival of the Europeans entered a period of crisis. Our independence was almost a gift, something we had not really earned. That is why we remained somewhat under the thumb of the ruling powers of the day.

We talk about the struggle for independence that took place between 1808 and 1825. It was not really a people's revolt, however. It was a revolt carried out by a Creole oligarchy who struggled to free themselves from Spain and then promptly fell under the sway of another empire. Today we talk about developed countries and underdeveloped countries. But the first and primary antithesis is really between traditional societies and developed societies. Traditional societies are those which are still independent because they have not yet felt the impact of a developed society. Such would be the Eskimos, the Pygmies, and the American Indians before the arrival of the Europeans. It is only when a traditional society is confronted with an advanced society that its people take cognizance of the gap that exists between the two. Only then do they begin to feel that they need something which they do not have. It is in this context that the notion of an underdeveloped society enters the picture.

Thus "underdeveloped" implies some sort of relationship with a "developed" society. It implies a situation where the "underdeveloped" party takes cognizance of the gap between it and the "developed" party. In that sense we can say that Latin America—not Amerindia—came into being as an "underdeveloped" society. When the conquistadores arrived, they realized that they were no longer in Spain, but they tried to re-create Spain here. Present-day Mexico was called New Spain, Colombia was called New Granada, and so forth. The label "New" suggested the attempt to re-create something here. Paradoxically enough, it also indicated that they were not building something new at all but rather something "old." They were trying to *repeat* and restore what they had left behind in Spain. And the society they had left behind was a much more developed one, so an awareness of underdevelopment marked our colonial society from the very beginning. Our society was an underdeveloped, dependent one because the whole structure of our economic, political, ecclesial, and cultural life was dependent on that of the great urban centers of Spain.

Spain dominated our colonial version of Christendom. It took our gold and silver to finance its operations against German Lutherans. And this gold and silver was obtained from the blood of our native Indians. Tainted with the injustice in effect here, the Catholic rulers and their administrators pleaded for money to carry out the great Catholic crusade against "the Lutheran heretics." Latin America lived within the totality of Spanish culture—aware of its underdeveloped situation and of its powerlessness. Its people were "oppressed."

This was the basic situation of our colonial Christendom, and it pervaded every level of life. Our philosophical and theological books came from Europe, and our theologians and philosophers felt honored to have their works published in Europe through Spain's influence.

The struggle for independence signified the revolt of the Creole oligarchy here against Spanish dominance. This group suffered most directly from the influence of Spain and wanted to free itself from that influence. It possessed very little real power in a system where Latin America was governed by a bureaucracy under the control of Spain—i.e., by officials of the *audiencias* and the *cabildos* ("town councils"), by viceroys and governors and bishops. It was this Creole class which rose up against Spain. Our "independence" movement in the nineteenth century was nothing more than a revolt by the Creole oligarchy. We must not forget that this Creole oligarchy also exercised domination—over the Indians and over the "little people" who were not part of its class. Thus most of the *mestizo* population possessed no power at all, and in the independence movement they served only as cannon fodder.

The Creole oligarchy broke with Spain because it was looking for a more advantageous pact, and it was the English who offered such a pact. Spain had taken gold and silver from Latin America and had offered wine and oil in return—even though these could be produced here. England, by contrast, offered manufactured products in return for our raw materials—under the basic system spelled out by Adam Smith. This new arrangement was agreed upon by our Creole oligarchy. Our "independence" was merely a switch from Spanish domination to domination by the new world power: industrial England. And our Creole oligarchy would take over the task of dominating people here.

This is the situation that prevailed in the nineteenth century. It continued into the twentieth century, although the name of the great foreign empire changed. Today it is the poor people of Latin America that hold our attention, for it is they who are now awakening to their situation. The process under way now is quite different from the one embodied in the revolutionary movements of the early nineteenth century, for it offers promise of effecting the liberation of the whole Latin American people from the dominance of foreign empires. We may be moving towards coexistence without dependence, towards a truly world culture in which each nation or people can contribute what is peculiarly its own.

What was the attitude of the Church towards the break effected in the early years of the nineteenth century? The bishops, for example, were realists to some extent. They tended to oppose the rupture with Spain and to opt for a

*58511*

return to the old situation of Spanish control. The clergy underneath them, however, were Creole for the most part—some even belonged to the oligarchy—and they threw themselves into the independence movement. Some took up arms, some organized armies (Hidalgo, Morelos), some melted down church bells for cannons (Fray Luis Beltrán). Slowly but surely the way was paved for complete independence from Spain in a process that had several stages.

After the first stirrings of revolt, Spain reacted and regained much of its control. By 1814 the Río de la Plata region was the only area that still remained independent from Spain. If Martín Güemes had not defended the northern boundary of Argentina against the Spanish armies, the destiny of Latin America might have turned out quite differently. Then a second thrust for independence began, with Bolívar operating in the north and San Martín in the south. Ultimately they came together at Guayaquil. In Mexico, the conservatives declared their independence from Spain because the liberals had gained control over the bureaucratic machinery of government. What is clear is that this whole transition took place within a basic framework of Catholic conservatism. There was no change in culture or in the pattern of existence, no real cultural or religious or theological break.

## THE DECADENCE CONTINUES IN A CONSERVATIVE MOLD (1825–1850)

During this next period we see a continuation of the structures that were already in existence. The new States were organized around some capital city or around the *audiencias* that had existed before. Central America began to split up into factions because there had always been a great deal of antagonism among the capital cities in that region. The history of San Salvador is very different from that of Guatemala, that of Costa Rica, and that of Panamá. Panamá, for example, belonged to Lima rather than to Mexico.

In this period, then, we see the forging of national unity in Latin America. Deterioration increased in the Church. The coming of independence meant the end of the system of *patronato*, so no missionaries came from Spain. No longer did books and money come from Spain either. In many areas not a single priest was ordained because there was no place for them to get training and no one to ordain them. And gradually a real rupture was beginning to appear.

In the northern part of New Spain, present-day southwestern United States was gradually taking form. Discov-

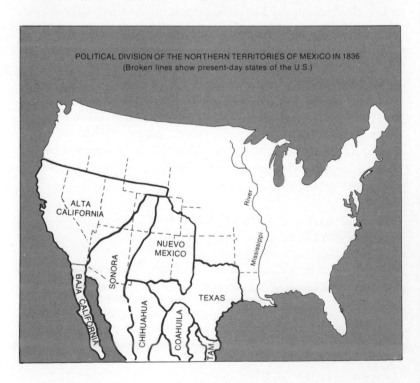

POLITICAL DIVISION OF THE NORTHERN TERRITORIES OF MEXICO IN 1836
(Broken lines show present-day states of the U.S.)

ered by Alvar Nuñez Cabeza de Vaca, it came to include the regions of Nuevo México, Nueva California, and San Luis Potosí (today stretching from Texas to California, Utah, Nevada, and Colorado). In 1803 Napoleon ceded Louisiana to the United States, marking the beginning of the doctrine of Manifest Destiny, under which the U.S. would extend its power all the way to the Pacific. The peaceful occupation of the area by the North Americans gradually occurred. The federalists of Mexico (including those of Yucatan and those to the north of the Rio Grande) meanwhile opposed the Mexican president Antonio López de Santa Ana. The North Americans fostered the federalist spirit, and the Texan revolution broke out in 1835–36. Santa Ana crushed the weak resistance at the Alamo, which was the occasion for Sam Houston to begin war and declare the independence of Texas (1836–45). Finally Mexico ceded the whole area, including California, to the U.S. (1848). In this way there emerged a Latin American people within the United States: the *nación* of the Spanish-speaking, a people who practically speaking have no Church and have been left to their "folk Catholicism."[4]

## RUPTURE TAKES PLACE (1850–1929)

The first liberal Constitution was promulgated in Colombia in 1849. A "new" America appeared on the scene and the colonial period was left behind. This Constitution proposed the separation of Church and State. Things had reached the point where certain minorities were able to implement doctrines that could not have been implemented previously. Real rupture with the Church began. The Church began to take a back seat, and even to fade out of the picture, because it could not respond to the challenges of the period. Yet the Church continued to have socio-political importance and to wield power. By virtue of their influence—not their economic power—the bishops were still important figures. Everyone still considered themselves Christians, and in fact they were after a fashion. But the elite were not Christian. They were of a liberal cast, leaning towards what would later take concrete shape as positivism.

The new government in Colombia (1849) was the first liberal government in Latin America. It was the first to declare itself anti-Christian, and anti-Catholic in particular. It would repudiate the Spanish past and Christendom. The liberals would write a new history, presenting the Spanish factor as a negative thing, rejecting colonial Catholicism, and denying the folk past. This step was taken in Colombia in 1849, in Argentina in 1853, and throughout Latin America during the 1850s.

From 1850 to 1929 we see the unfolding of a whole new project in Latin America, a project sponsored by a liberal oligarchy rather than by a conservative one. In general we could say that it looked to France for its cultural ideals and to the United States for its technological ideals. It was in these places that it would find its concrete historical ideals, rejecting our past as a period of barbarism.

Around 1870 positivism became the dominant ideology, thanks to such men as José Ingenieros in Argentina and Miguel Lemos in Brazil. This "atheistic" materialism was actually an anti-creationist materialism which affirmed the divinity of matter. In short, it was pantheism. It imposed itself on our culture during this period (1870–1890), and our lawyers and doctors are still formed under its influence.

This bourgeois oligarchy, which did not actually possess a great deal of power, was anticlerical and anti-Catholic. The crisis encountered by the system known as Christendom was thus due to a variety of factors: the Church's lack of resources, the absence of bishops, the disappearance of seminaries, the cessation of shipments of priests and books

from Spain, and a planned rupture put through systematically by the ruling oligarchy. The oligarchy in power was
fundamentally anti-Catholic.

The Church could hardly respond to the new challenge.
There was not only a missionary crisis but also a theological
crisis in Europe. Only towards the end of the nineteenth
century would Mercier begin the work of philosophical and
theological renewal that would usher in the third version of
scholasticism. And even this was unable to respond to Darwin, Comte, and Marx. The Church seemed to be on the
verge of disappearing. Indeed it may have been a more
serious crisis than the one we face today.

The new and rising bourgeois oligarchy was a latecomer
on the industrial scene, however. The crisis of 1929 proved
to be fatal to it, and it lost its political power. Let us consider
why this happened. When Adam Smith's book, *An Inquiry
into the Nature and Causes of the Wealth of Nations,* was published in 1776, the British bourgeois oligarchy enjoyed the
advantages of overall social peace. They could organize
industry and exploit the workers because the workers did
not have the image of some other working class that was
better off. The British worker labored eighteen hours a day
in the factory, and so did all European workers. Thus the
bourgeoisie had time to take advantage of this exploitation
and to increase its capital. Business enterprises grew slowly
and steadily, and so did the worker; industrial society had
time to mature and develop into an affluent entity. By
contrast, our industrial bourgeoisie arrived on the scene
around 1890. The Latin American worker would not labor
eighteen hours a day because he knew that workers elsewhere worked only ten hours. Thus a contradiction appeared in the system, because the Latin American worker
would make demands which the Latin American industrial
system could not yet afford to meet. If it met these demands, it would not be able to sink money back into the

system and keep it going. The crisis in 1929 proved fatal to this bourgeois elite in Latin America, and in 1930 a new power influence would break in.

## THE ATTEMPT TO BUILD A "NEW CHRISTENDOM"

1930 was a key year throughout Latin America. Catholicism gained breathing space when the anti-Catholic liberal class lost power. Catholic Action was gradually implemented throughout the continent, and an attempt to revive Catholicism as a "new Christendom" got under way. The laity appeared once again; and in place of the oligarchy that once had dominated, the military class came to the fore.

I refer to this new effort as an attempt to fashion a "new" Christendom. The revitalized scholasticism of the time permitted one to envision only a renewal or imitation of the Christian culture that had once existed. Maritain's *Integral Humanism* spoke in such terms. Since Latin Americans knew almost nothing about their colonial period, the only image they had was one of medieval Christendom. Writers such as Leon Bloy and Hilaire Belloc were read by many Catholics. People wanted to restore the Christendom that had almost disappeared during the period of liberal persecution.

Thus began the great effort at reconquest on the part of Catholicism. It sought to be triumphant and to dominate education, politics, and even economics. In effect it was a triumphalist effort. Catholic Action and the Christian Democratic Party would dominate until Vatican II. I am not going to suggest that the postconciliar Church is a different entity or Church. It is the same Church going through its inner process of growth. The essential elements would continue to grow during the course of time.

The effort to establish a new Christendom would gradually begin to show weak points. Both Catholic Action and the Christian Democratic Party would begin to falter. Writing from Brazil, Belgian theologian Joseph Comblin pointed out the failure of Catholic Action. Comblin's book (*Echec de l'action catholique?*) proved to be a bombshell, even though it really points up the limitations rather than the failure of Catholic Action.

## THE WORLDWIDE CRISIS OF CHRISTIAN CULTURES

The Russian version of Byzantine Christendom received a fatal blow in 1917. The rest of Europe had begun a process of secularization several centuries earlier. This secularization process gradually turned into "secularism." What started out as a process to give proper autonomy to the temporal sphere became an anti-Christian philosophy.

Many men of the Church had been spending their time defending Christendom as a culture rather than Christianity as a religion. They defended the cultural influence of the Church and eventually the papal states. Defense of the papal states is deeply interwoven into Vatican I, the Council which took place in the latter half of the nineteenth century. The Church was deeply concerned about the fact that Italian "libertines" wanted to attack the papal states. Today we have regained a healthy measure of liberty, much in the same way that ancient Israel did in the Babylonian exile: through poverty and persecution.

In Hispano-America, anticlerical liberalism and positivism were the instruments of divine providence. Secularization, laicism, and secularism helped to restore some degree of liberty to the Church.

## THE PRESENT SITUATION

As we noted earlier, Vatican II ushered in a third stage in Church history. Some people had anticipated this new stage in their thinking, and on the whole they fared badly. Lagrange, the great Dominican exegete, carried on his fine biblical work in an atmosphere of persecution. Teilhard de Chardin worked in silence. And the case was much the same with Yves Congar.

In 1937 Congar wrote a book on separated Christians (Eng. trans.: *Divided Christendom*, London, 1939). If one picks up that book today, it seems hardly novel. But at the time it was a dangerous book and its reprinting was forbidden. The great school of Le Saulchoir was liquidated, and the *nouvelle théologie* was attacked. This "new theology" was really nothing more than a sound "historical" theology. But it was torn apart, as Congar himself has told me, and its proponents were scattered. The possibility of teamwork, centered around a great library, was wiped out.

With Vatican II we certainly enter a new stage: the manifestation of Christianity on an extensive scale to mankind all over the world, to all the cultures that had never yet been evangelized. European civilization, that is, technological civilization, is now worldwide, and this fact poses a serious question: Will all the cultures of the world be unified into one and only one culture—a culture based on the experiences of only one segment of mankind? There is no doubt that cultures are confronting each other as never before, and it seems possible that only one will survive the confrontation. It is a serious matter.

The Church exists in history, and it too is challenged by the confrontation between cultures. But it may well be that a process of pre-evangelization is going on even though we have not adverted to the fact. As we noted earlier, Ricci did not manage to evangelize China. England did not conquer China in the Opium War either. Suddenly we find, however, that a Chinese Marxist has Europeanized China. It is now difficult to read the works of Confucius in China, but very easy to read the works of Karl Marx, a European philosopher who grew up in the Judeo-Christian tradition.

The same process may be at work in Hindu and Muslim culture. The introduction of Western technology into these cultures may well bring about a theological crisis. What will Hinduism do if slaughterhouses are imported into its territories? What will the theocratic Muslim states do in the face of other contemporary governments which are lay in nature? The Christian religion does not have problems with these realities, whereas Hinduism and Islamism do.

Let me sum up my main point here. Christendom—that vast cultural, religious, and socio-political reality of the past—is on its way out. That is the reason behind all the critical problems we as Christians are now facing in Latin America. Some want to hold on to Christendom, but time spent on seeking to preserve Christendom is so much time lost for Christianity.

## NOTES

1. On Bartolomé de Las Casas, see the fine work of Manuel Giménez Fernández, *Bartolomé de las Casas* (Seville: EEHS, 1953–60).

2. See my *Historia de la Iglesia en América Latina*. Further bibliographical material can be found in that work.

3. See the two volumes on *Santo Toribio de Mogrovejo* by Vicente Rodríguez Valencia (Madrid: CSIC, 1956–57).

4. For a bibliography on the "Chicanos" or "Mexican Americans" (or simply "Hispanic groups," since some of the descendents of the Spaniards in this area do not accept the other labels), see Wayne Moquin and Charles Van Doren, eds., *A Documentary History of the Mexican Americans* (New York: Praeger, 1971); Matthew Meier and Feliciano Rivera, *The Chicanos: A History of Mexican Americans* (New York: Hill and Wang, 1972); Rudy Acuna, *Occupied America: The Chicano's Struggle Toward Liberation* (San Francisco: Canfield Press, 1972).

# 4

# Significant Events
# of the Last Decade (1962–1972)

In this chapter we shall take a look at some of the events that have taken place since 1962. By examining them we may be able to form some judgment about what is happening today.

## VATICAN II (1962–1965)

Recent as it was, Vatican II seems to lie far behind us because so much has happened in Latin America in the past decade. It is almost as if a century of history had been crammed into this short space of time. Indeed the participation—or lack of participation—of Latin American bishops in previous Councils is itself suggestive. One bishop at the Lateran Council of 1517 would later be bishop of Santo Domingo.[1] This bishop, Alejandro de Geraldini, happened to be in Rome at the time waiting for his formal nomination. He had not yet set foot in Latin America, but he was the first American bishop to attend an ecumenical council. There were sixty-five Latin American bishops at Vatican I, but they did not take an active role and merely approved what Rome proposed. Some German partici-pants and in particular the "Old Catholics" were shocked by the seeming ignorance of these representatives from the "new" Churches of Latin America. The fact that the Churches of Latin America were hardly "new" compared to those in Africa and elsewhere did not register with some people—including the Church historian, Johannes Döllinger.

At Vatican II, the Latin American presence was much more substantial, even though it might well have been even greater in proportionate terms. Over six hundred Latin American bishops were present at the Council: i.e., 22 percent of the total. But the Catholic population of Latin America is 38 percent of the world Catholic population—hence considerably more than was proportionately represented at the Council. The difference shows up even more clearly in the study commissions. There were only fifty Latin American *periti* on the staff of these commissions. Europe, which has about the same Catholic population, had 219 *periti*. Rome had 318 *periti*, six times the number of *periti* from Latin America. Latin American influence disappeared almost completely in the executive organs of the Council.

There was one Latin American, Cardinal Antonio Caggiano of Buenos Aires, on the presiding board of the Council. It was Cardinal Achille Liénart of Lille, however, who really got the Council started. He himself has described to me what happened. When he was presented with the agenda for the Council, he noticed that everything seemed to have been organized and fixed in advance. When it came time for him to speak, he simply voiced what he felt without stopping to think about its possible impact. He said in Latin, "Mihi non placet." There was a thunderous burst of applause, and the Council began in earnest. It was the same sensitivity and awareness that Liénart had displayed back in 1930. He was in conflict with the business owners of Lille, and the latter requested that he be replaced. The Pope refused to do that; instead he made him a Cardinal when he was little more than forty-five years old.

Manuel Larraín, the Bishop of Talca, was the Latin American who exerted the most influence at the Council. He was never made a cardinal, but this great Chilean bishop certainly should have been one by virtue of his longstanding involvement in Catholic Action and his work for land reform in Chile. Many other bishops made their presence felt at the Council, but I would say that the involvement of the Latin American bishops could have been much greater. At any rate they did get to meet each other and to talk things over; and they had a chance to meet with other bishops from underdeveloped countries. One very interesting result of such meetings and conversations was the message issued by the bishops of the Third World to their peoples.[2] Dom Helder Camara of Brazil headed the list of signatories, and the message itself proclaimed that the peoples of the Third World were the proletariat of today's world. It also spoke on themes connected with the international imperialism of money. This text would subsequently have an impact on the Medellín Conference. But the fact remains that Vatican II itself was a reflection of postwar European neocapitalism.

THE MEDELLIN CONFERENCE (1968)

The Medellín Conference was the Second General Conference of the Latin American Episcopate. The first such conference had taken place in Río de Janeiro (1955), where the Latin American Episcopal Conference (CELAM) was formed. The Medellín Conference might well be considered the Vatican II of Latin America, even as the Third Council of Lima (1582–83) is often considered the Latin American Trent.

It was the Medellín Conference that gave concrete form and application to Vatican II. The result was somewhat of a surprise, because a previous meeting had not produced much in the way of results and an air of scepticism surrounded the upcoming meeting. The visit of Pope Paul VI to Latin America, however, alerted public opinion and created an atmosphere of hopefulness. His speeches in Latin America touched upon some key ideas and also helped to stir the thinking of our own bishops. He noted that "broad and courageous vision" would be required to put through the reforms "necessary for a more just and efficient social arrangement." He exhorted the people of Latin America not to place their trust in violence and revolution: "That is contrary to the Christian spirit, and can even delay, rather than advance, that social uplifting to which you lawfully aspire." It was a theme to which he returned: "Many . . . insist on the need for urgent change in social structures . . . and some conclude that Latin America's essential problem can be solved only by violence. . . . We must say and reaffirm that violence is not in accord with the Gospel, that it is not Christian."[3]

These texts were interpreted within the overall context of his other addresses and encyclicals, and commentaries were worked up by various figures: Father Alfonso Gregory of Brazil; Bishop Marcos MacGrath of Panamá; Bishop Eduardo Pironio of CELAM; Bishop Samuel Ruíz of Chiapas, Mexico; Bishop Pablo Muñoz Vega of Ecuador; Bishop Luis Henríquez of Venezuela; and Bishop Leonidas Proaño of Riobamba, Ecuador. In the discussions and preparatory documents of the Medellín Conference, the teaching of Vatican II and the popes was fleshed out in terms of the Latin American situation. The *Conclusions* gave voice to a new tone and a new idiom in the language of the Latin American Church: "It is the same God who, in the fullness of time, sends his Son in the flesh, so that he might come to liberate all men from the slavery to which sin has subjected them: hunger, misery, oppression, and ignorance, in a word, that injustice and hatred which have their origin in human selfishness."[4] And it went on to spell out some of the concrete implications of such a vision. Here is one example:

"As the Christian believes in the productiveness of peace in order to achieve justice, he also believes that justice is a prerequisite for peace. He recognizes that in many instances Latin America finds itself faced with a situation of injustice that can be called institutionalized violence. ... This situation demands all-embracing, courageous, urgent, and profoundly renovating transformations. We should not be surprised, therefore, that the 'temptation to violence' is surfacing in Latin America. One should not abuse the patience of a people that for years has borne a situation that would not be acceptable to anyone with any degree of awareness of human rights."[5]

These documents of the Medellín Conference speak in the idiom of liberation, talking about such matters as dependence, domination, and the international imperialism of money. Yet the thought of that Conference stands somewhere in the transitional phase between "developmentalism" and the "theology of liberation." Starting with the basic fact of a gap between the "developed" and the "underdeveloped" countries, the developmentalist approach suggests that the underdeveloped countries must catch up to the former countries by more or less imitating their way of doing things. This approach tended to dominate our thinking in the 60s, and it is still evident in the thinking of the Medellín Conference. As time went on, however, it became evident that the underdeveloped countries could never catch up with the developed nations by adopting that approach. The gap between the two types grows greater every day. The belatedly industrialized countries cannot gain their economic independence simply by following in the footsteps of the "advanced" nations. The price of manufactured products increases steadily while the price of raw materials provided by the underdeveloped countries declines. The resultant economic and political problems have gradually made their impact felt in the field of theology also.

If the underdeveloped countries are to attain liberation, they must break the cycle of dependence on advanced industrialized countries. This fact began to be seen more clearly right after the Medellín Conference, and theologians began to talk about a new model for the underdeveloped nations. Tying in this model with biblical thinking, they began to talk about a "theology of liberation." It was Augusto Salazar Bondy, a Peruvian philosopher, who called our attention to the fact that the domination exerted over us was not only economic and political but also cultural in the broad sense. His work attracted the attention of Gustavo Gutiérrez, who has done much to spell out the basic underpinnings of liberation theology.[6] We shall return to this whole matter in the next chapter. Right now I should like to sketch some of the reactions of the Church and Christians to recent events in Latin America.

## THE COUPS D'ETAT IN BRAZIL AND PERU

Between 1962 and 1972 there have been significant political overthrows in Latin America. The coups in Brazil (1964), Argentina (1966), and Peru (1968) were major events because they affected more than half of the total Latin American population. Towards these events the Church adopted different and sometimes contradictory stances, and I should like to touch on those which occurred in Brazil and Peru as examples of what is going on.

The Church had organized various social movements in Brazil before Goulart was deposed and the military junta took over. One of the most interesting was the development movement in Natal, which was concerned with the growth of the northeast section of the country. This movement, known as SUDENE (*Superintendencia del Desenvolvimiento del N.E.*), eventually would end in failure, but basically it was a continuation of the peasant leagues (*Ligas camponesas*) of Francisco Juliao. There would also begin in Brazil the movement for basic education (MEB) based on the approach of Paulo Freire. The Church was progressively making its presence known in Brazilian society. The weakness of the Goulart government paved the way for the military coup of March 31, 1964, and a new phase began in the life of that nation.

Twelve days after the military coup Dom Helder Camara, a friend of Paul VI, was nominated Bishop of Olinda and Recife. He had been in Rome when the bishop of a small diocese in Brazil died. Paul VI wanted to make him the bishop of a diocese, but he also wanted him to take over a larger and more important one. Right around that time the bishop of Olinda and Recife also died, and Camara was nominated to replace him.

On April 12, 1964, Dom Helder Camara delivered an address which, in my opinion, was one of the most forthright theological statements ever made in Latin American history. It was truly prophetic, in the tradition of men like Montesinos. Camara is a prophet and a poet who uses a dialectical approach which we shall explore in detail in the next chapter. He began this way: "I am a native of northeast Brazil, speaking to other natives of that region, with my gaze focused on Brazil, Latin America, and the world. I speak as a human being, in fellowship with the frailty and sinfulness of all other human beings; as a Christian to other Christians, but with a heart open to all individuals, peoples, and ideologies; as a bishop of the Catholic Church who, like Christ, seeks to serve rather than be served. May my fraternal greeting be heard by all: Catholics and non-Catholics, believers and non-believers. Praised be Jesus Christ!"[7]

No clearer statement has been made since Vatican II. Camara takes his standpoint as a native of his own region, and then lets his horizons open up to encompass broader realities. His is a truly "catholic" vision encompassing the whole world, the eschatological totality of the kingdom.

The concluding remarks of his address are truly pro-

phetic ones: "It would be wrong to suppose that our opposition to atheistic communism implies a defense of liberal
capitalism. It would be erroneous to conclude that we are
communist because we as Christians vigorously criticize the
egotistical position of economic liberalism." This is the classic stance of the Christian prophet. He will oppose the
unjust use of power and bourgeois liberalism, but he will
also oppose orthodox Marxism. The latter is unacceptable
because it is atheistic—or rather, pantheistic, as we have
noted earlier. It turns its own world into an absolute whole
and denies the Other. It ends up denying God and propos-
ing a fatal, egotistical totalitarianism.

The Christian is forced to move forward in history, buf-
feted by the storm around him and removed from the
established order. As Jesus said to Pilate: "My kingdom is
not of this world." In other words, the Christian keeps
moving into the future, drawing the whole process of history in his wake. He fights and struggles for the poor, and
the poor do not have any institutions to defend them.
Hence he must die as a martyr for the kingdom.

It seems to me that there have been great figures in the
various stages of Latin American Church history. In the
early colonial period there was Bartolomé de Las Casas and
Toribio de Mogrovejo. In the nineteenth century there was
Bishop Mariano Casanova, and then the long line of great
Chilean bishops which culminated with Bishop Larraín. In
the last decade we have figures like Dom Helder Camara in
Brazil and Sergio Méndez Arceo, the Bishop of Cuernavaca, Mexico.

On May 7, 1964, Tristão de Atayde spoke out in the pages
of the *Folha de Sao Paulo*. In his youth he had been a great
student of Maritain but, unlike the latter, he did not back-
track on his opinions in later years. Unlike the author of the
*Peasant of the Garonne*, he continued to follow the process of
history even in his later years. In his article, he spoke out
against the cultural terrorism that had taken over in Brazil.

What else is it, he asked, "when men of international stature are deprived of their posts . . . simply because they express opinions contrary to the new prevailing ideology; when purely metaphysical philosophers arc jailed . . . along with young intellectuals simply because their methods of teaching literacy are regarded as subversive; when the organs of Catholic Action . . . are exhorted to abstain from activities that are 'incompatible with the interests of the nation and its people' as if they were under the tutelage of the State?"

My point here is a simple one. Our young people sometimes wonder where we will find martyrs to match those of old. Well, we may not have had them for awhile, but there have been many, indeed hundreds, in Latin America in the last ten years. And there probably will be many more. A clear case in point is the young priest of the diocese of Olinda y Recife in Brazil, who was assassinated at the age of twenty-eight. His life was threatened, but he continued his work as adviser to a Catholic Action group of university students. On the night of May 27, 1969, he was abducted, tortured, stripped, tied to a stake, and shot. This young priest, Henrique Pereira Neto, was a martyr as surely as any in the Roman empire. And there have been many others like him in Latin America. Something extraordinary and important is going on in our lands.

When the average European of today utters a prayer, he or she does it calmly and simply. Only once or twice in a lifetime is the European faced with a critical choice that will affect his or her whole life. The European decides to pursue a certain line of work, to get married, to enter the religious life. After that, life goes on for forty or fifty years without any life-or-death option entering the picture. The moral intensity of life is experienced in one or two moments. In Latin America, by contrast, we may be faced with life-or-death options over and over again. It is happening in Brazil, and we must face the reality of the situation.

A military government also took over in Peru in 1968, but

it began to tackle things in a very different manner. The Church, too, adopted a different posture when faced with the new situation. The new military government adopted a nationalistic policy that entailed some degree of socializing the economic capacity of the country. A say in the government was granted to Christians and to others who have been traditionally anti-Christian: e.g., socialists and communists. Towards this policy the Church has adopted a very positive attitude—quite in contrast to the situation in Brazil.

Up to 1962, in short, the Church tended to defend its own rights and its own institutions vis-à-vis the State. Since then the Church has tended to defend the rights of the poor and the common people, the Other, and the ensuing conflicts stem mainly from that fact. A radical change in attitude has taken place, more akin to the pro-Indian attitude of some colonial bishops.

## THE CHURCH CONFRONTS SOCIALISM IN CUBA

I want to consider briefly the situation of the Church in Cuba since Castro's forces entered Havana on January 8, 1959. Initial relations between Castro and the Church were very cordial, but estrangement soon set in. By February of 1960 Castro was saying that anyone opposed to communism was also opposed to the revolution. The Church began to take a stance openly against the government, and this trend culminated in a statement by the Cuban episcopate on August 7, 1960: "Let no one ask us Catholics to silence our opposition to such doctrines out of a false sense of civil loyalty. We cannot agree to that without betraying our deepest principles, which are opposed to materialistic and atheistic communism. The vast majority of the Cuban people are Catholic, and only by deceit can they be won over to a communist regime." Open persecution then began. By 1970 the number of nuns in Cuba had dropped from 1200 to 200, the number of diocesan priests from 745 to 230. For almost ten years it was a Church of silence.

Then Bishop Cesare Zacchi, who had long experience in socialist countries, was appointed Apostolic Nuncio to Cuba. He made it clear that another attitude was possible. The Church changed its stance, and subsequently the government did also. The prime minister of Cuba would admit that an entirely new situation was at hand: "We are faced with a paradox of history. When we see many priests becoming a force for revolution, how can we resign ourselves to seeing Marxist sectors infected with an ecclesiastical kind of conservatism?" The whole situation would have been unthinkable a few short years before. The attitude of the Church began to change, particularly after Medellín.

On April 10, 1969, the Cuban episcopate issued a statement in which it denounced the economic blockade of Cuba: "In the interests of our people and in service to the poor, faithful to the mandate of Jesus Christ and the commitments made at the Medellín Conference, we denounce the injustice of this blockade. For it causes a great increase in unnecessary suffering, and greatly impedes the quest for development." This message marked the start of a new phase in which the problem of contemporary atheism was faced directly. A statement of September 3, 1969, explored the issue in concrete terms: "In the betterment of the whole man and of all mankind there is an enormous area of shared commitment between people of good will, be they atheists or believers." It noted the critical importance of every moment in history: "In this hour, as in every hour, we must be wise enough to detect the presence of God's kingdom in the positive features of the critical situation through which we are living."

The thought of the Cuban episcopate is crystal clear. Their words reveal a true prophetic sense and a vital faith. The Church of Cuba is going through a crisis and facing up to it; it will not have to face that crisis in some future century. If one faces up to the crisis of today, he will be over the worst when tomorrow comes.

Here I cannot review the older revolution which took place in Mexico and the attitude of Christians during it. But I do want to say something about Chile, even though I must be very brief and overlook recent happenings. The important point to note here is that the Church did not set itself up in adamant opposition to the socialist government of Allende and the Popular Front. The episcopate continued the process of dialogue to see where and how things would go. Moreover, substantial groups of Christians participated in the Popular Front coalition.

In this respect Chileans have demonstrated much more maturity than other Christians when it comes to politics. In 1936 a group of Christians left the Conservative Party to form the Christian Democratic Party. Members of the latter left to form MAPU [Movimiento de Acción Popular Unido, United Movement for Peoples' Action], a Marxist party composed of Christians, which took part in the Popular Front. And some members of MAPU left that party to form MIC [Movimiento Izquierdista Cristiano, Movement of the Christian Left], a leftist but non-Marxist party of Christian socialists. I think this distinction between a Marxist party made up of Christians and a non-Marxist party of Christian socialists will be most important in the immediate future of Latin America.

## THE REALITY OF VIOLENCE
## IN LATIN AMERICA

The physiognomy of events is different to some extent in every country of Latin America, but we cannot explore every country here. So let us try to examine the problem of violence in terms of a couple of countries.

Colombia is a country in which violence has reigned since the first days of Spanish conquest. The conquistadores slaughtered Indians in wholesale fashion as they went about looking for gold. One bishop noted that the Indians had come to assume that gold was the god of the Spaniard, and they had reason. Gold was almost an idol for many Spaniards, and they went about sacking Chibcha tombs to find it. The Chibchas buried gold objects with their dead, and the Spaniards desecrated their burial areas in search of the wealth which was needed in Spain to combat the "Lutheran heretics."

Violence-ridden Colombia is also the Colombia which produced a most significant figure in the last decade. I cannot explore his whole history here,[8] but I must allude to the basic outlines of his intellectual and spiritual itinerary. Camilo Torres received his degree in sociology from the University of Louvain. Four months before his death he expressed his admiration for dedicated Marxists but noted that he would never join their ranks: "They are sincerely seeking the truth and they love their neighbor in an efficacious way, but they must know very well that I will never enter their ranks. I will never be a communist—neither as a Colombian, a sociologist, a Christian, or a priest."

Camilo Torres was an intelligent Christian who confronted sociology, history, and his faith in his own way. One ideal dominated his thinking and writing: *love*. He believed it was the one and only Christian commandment, but he also believed it had to be *efficacious* love. This thought, which appears repeatedly in his writings and statements, gradually effected a change in his own approach and life. In 1963, for example, he wrote these negative comments on violence: "Violence has effected all these changes through pathological channels which in no way dovetail with the country's process of economic development." He was opposed to violence, yet gradually this attitude would change.

The Church displayed a lack of comprehension which gradually shackled him. The university professor was prevented from becoming university rector. He was asked to withdraw his name from the nominations for the post. Then he was asked to stop speaking and writing. Desiring to pursue the demands of his Christian faith, he asked to be laicized so that he might be involved in politics; but the doors of the political world were closed to him. He was shunted aside and gradually forced to make a definitive commitment. And then his corpse was found. We do not know for sure whether he died as a guerrilla fighter, or whether he was assassinated first and then passed off as such.

When we read some of his writings, we cannot help but think of some of the earlier bishops and other present-day martyrs. He wrote: "After analyzing Colombian society. I have come to the conclusion that a revolution is necessary if we are to feed the hungry, clothe the naked, and bring well-being to the majority of our people. The supreme gauge of our decisions should be charity: supernatural love. I will take all the risks that this ideal imposes on me." It is the underlying attitude of such men as Valdivieso, who was assassinated by Contreras; Pereira Neto, who was killed on his way to a meeting of Catholic Action; and Father Hector Gallegos of Panama, who was first threatened and then killed for his work with peasant cooperatives. Since we have not yet given our own lives, we must respect those who did.

The situation in Guatemala is depicted in powerful terms by Thomas Melville, who was a Maryknoll missioner there. His words speak for themselves: "During the last eighteen months, these three rightist groups have slain more than 2800 people: intellectuals, students, union and peasant leaders, and others who have tried in one way or another to organize the people and combat the evils of Guatemalan society. I personally know a man, a good friend and daily communicant, who accused a Christian union leader of being a communist because he was trying to organize a union in his sugar plantation. He thus got him shot by the army. When the cooperative I had organized among the Indians of Quezaltenango was finally able to buy its own truck, the rich people tried to bribe the driver so that he would wreck the vehicle. He refused their overtures, so they tried several times to force him off the road and over a cliff. They were successful on the fourth try. In the parish of San Antonio Huista where my brother—also a Maryknoller—was pastor, the president of the agrarian cooperative was assassinated by the people in power—the mayor included. When the case was brought to the capital city of Huehuetenango, the judge had already been bought off and nothing came of it."

Melville goes on to say: "The American government has sent jeeps, helicopters, armaments, doctors, and military advisers to the government in power. This merely strengthens their control over the peasant masses. In 1967 salaries, uniforms, arms, and vehicles for two thousand additional police were paid for by the Alliance For Progress. When twenty-five priests got together to organize farm workers on the large haciendas along the southern coast, the bishops of Huehuetenango, San Marcos, Quezaltenango and Sololá dispatched a harsh letter forbidding us to get involved in such a project. It said that it was none of our business, and that we should be content with preaching the Gospel message."[9]

Hundreds of comments of this sort could be presented here. But instead I want to reflect briefly on the whole matter of violence in the Latin American context.

When Cain killed Abel, he set up a "totality" in which the Other came to be at best a slave under his domination. Everything goes well so long as the slave does not advert to his situation or feel any self-worth. If I feel I am worth nothing, it is because I have been subjected to a pedagogy that has driven that point home to me. But if I suddenly begin to think that I am worth something, if I suddenly place myself outside the totality fashioned by my master and oppressor, then a process of liberation begins and the situation becomes quite serious. The oppressor will try to prevent me from taking the step to freedom; he will try to keep me in his totality by force. This is what Dom Helder Camara calls the "first violence." It is the violence of an unjust situation which prevents the reified man from being free. This first sin is the gravest of all because it reifies human beings, turning them into things. The person en route to freedom, the person in the "exodus," must defend himself from this first violence.

The defense is just. It seeks to prevent the exercise of a violence that would keep the process of liberation from taking place. The Jesuit Reductions in Paraguay offer us an example here. The Jesuits organized the Indians of the Gran Chaco area into civilized communities. Then colonists came and attacked these Indians, robbing them and killing them. The Jesuits asked the king for permission to arm the Indians. The king did not want to grant this permission, but they went ahead and armed the Indians. The incursions stopped, and the Jesuit Reductions went on existing for at least a century and a half. When the Jesuits left, the Indians gradually lost their supply of arms. Soon the Reductions were no more. It is sad to visit the ruins of those edifices today, which were really destroyed by the "first violence" of which I spoke above. The Jesuit defense of the Indians was the defense of the Other, of the poor.

If someone wants to kill my child, I am not going to let him. If the aggressor has a knife, then I must get a knife to defend the child. If I do not, then I am an irresponsible parent. I am committing a sin.

So there is a "first violence": organized, legal violence. And there is a "second" violence: the violence that sets out to establish a new "whole." The second violence is the violence of San Martín, for example. He organized his soldiers and followers. When the Spaniards came to destroy the new homeland, he went out to fight them—paving the way for a new whole that is present-day Argentina. If that conflict had not taken place, there would not be any Argentina today.

Thomas Aquinas never said that force as such is evil. He said that force, like all the passions, is equivocal. The essential question is: For what purpose are they used? If I love something, but it truly belongs to another, then I commit a sin. If I love my neighbor as such, however, that is very fine indeed. "Violence" is associated with the Latin word *vis*, which means "strength" or "force" or "power." I may use "violence" or "force"—not that of arms, needless to say—to preach the Gospel message; such was the "violence" of the prophets, for example. In short, the "second violence" of which we spoke above can be virtue insofar as it is the defense of the Other. The "first violence," however, is always sinful. It is the violence of unjust law and established disorder. If the Christian opposes violence, then he must oppose all violence. In particular, he must oppose the "first violence," which is the violence of the pharaoh rather than that of the plagues.

This justification of violence is a theological and ineradicable aspect of the Christian faith. Many passages from the Church Fathers and other theologians could be introduced to prove the point. Thomas Aquinas justified the death penalty; Saint Bernard justified crusades to recapture the Lord's sepulcher in Israel; Christians have waged many wars in defense of what they regarded as their just rights. I am not suggesting that all these wars were truly in defense of the poor, of course. Christian crusaders sacked and exploited Byzantium when they went to recapture the holy sepulcher. That was not virtue but injustice.

But there is also the violence of the spoken word, the violence of the prophet and martyr. It is the distinctive and peculiar violence of the Church as such. Violence in defense of a new political order is not the proper violence of the Church as such, even though it may be proper to the committed Christian individual. The Church as such is a prophetic body which dies for the sake of the Other but which, as Church, never kills anyone. In the throes of his passion and death, Jesus pardoned his persecutors. That is the only way to respect one's persecutor as a human being. If I abuse or insult him, then I am treating him as a thing. I must realize that he does not know what he is doing; if he did, he would not do it.

## THE ATTITUDE OF BISHOPS AND PRIESTS

The Chilean episcopate provided the model for Latin America in the decades which preceded Vatican II. Since Vatican II, it is the Brazilian episcopate that has pointed out the road for us. They have found themselves at a very difficult crossroad, and many of them have played an important role. Among them, of course, stands Dom Helder Camara.

His life has been most interesting. He is the son of a public school teacher, and hence he grew up in an educational atmosphere. He was ordained at the age of twenty-three, and was immediately entrusted with a task that was practically political in nature. Certain parties had agreed to include the Church and its rights in their program, and Helder Camara was to serve as the spokesman of the Church in connection with these groups. Being a great organizer, he did much to shape the whole structure of this coalition. Afterwards he was appointed Minister of Education in his own province, and then later in Rio de Janeiro. In short, up to the age of thirty he spent most of his working life in civil organisms of the State.

Camara got the idea of organizing an episcopal conference in Brazil. He went to speak to the papal Secretary of

State, who would later become Paul VI. The papal Secretary of State liked the idea and appointed Camara Secretary of the new organism.

In 1955 Cardinal Gerlier of Lyons, a great missionary bishop in the tradition of Liénart and Suhard, asked Camara why he did not turn his organizing talents to the whole problem of the slums, the Brazilian *favelas*. It was Gerlier's questioning that awoke the social conscience of Camara, as he himself has admitted.

The Brazilian episcopate is an exemplary one, and so it is not surprising that there have not been many priestly protest movements in Brazil. The top leadership has led the way, and the rest have followed. The lack of episcopal leadership in Argentina, on the other hand, explains why one of the major priestly movements in Latin America arose there: the movement of Priests for the Third World.[10] The history of the Church in the Argentinian nation has been very conformist. Rarely if ever has it broken new ground or played a prophetic role. But this priestly movement is truly something new and extraordinary in Argentina.

The beginning of this priestly group goes back to meetings that took place in 1965 and 1966. At them priests discussed Vatican II's pastoral constitution on the Church in the World of Today (*Gaudium et spes*), and the message of eighteen bishops from the Third World. The press referred to the discussion group as "Priests for the Third World," and the name stuck when it officially organized in Córdoba, Argentina, on May 1, 1968.

The most important fact about this movement is that its members are exploring new ways to live the priestly life. The secular priesthood is the ecclesial institution which is most severely affected by the difficulties of the present-day situation. Bishops and members of religious orders have a certain "internal" environment within the Church which enables them, to a certain extent, to forget the outside world and its problems. The layman may suffer exclusion from the Church if he chooses to live his life in certain ways, but his life will still go on as before. The one who is caught in the middle is really the simple priest. He is a man of the Church, yet he is directly confronted with the world situation too. It is in connection with the institution of the priesthood that the most difficult problems have arisen during the course of Church history, and it is there that the most basic crisis is evident today.

In a strident article Ivan Illich has voiced the opinion that we shall soon see the end of the clerical state ("The Vanishing Clergyman," *Critic*, June-July 1967). His point is that within the context of what I have called "Christendom" the priesthood has been a profession similar to other accepted professions. But once Christianity separates itself from this cultural setting and prophetically confronts secular society, the clerical "profession" will no longer be a real possibility. The priest will have some other profession, but he will also officiate as a pastor of souls at the liturgy. The clerical *status* will disappear in the secular city, and indeed the process has been going on for some time already. It is evident among the priests who belong to the Argentinian movement, among priests in Peru who are part of the ONIS group, among the Golconda group in Colombia, and among the priests who were members of the Christians for Socialism movement in Chile. In all these groups we can see an attempt to explore and redefine the priestly function in the Church and world of today.

The Roman Synod of 1971 discussed some secondary aspects of this whole question. The question itself, however, will persist for some years to come because the priestly institution is a central one. Only a solid theology of the ministry will be able to point out a pathway that is truly missionary and prophetic.

## CHANGING STRUCTURES
## AND THE ATTITUDE OF THE LAITY

In this section and the next one I want to say something about the attitude of the laity towards events which have taken place in the last few years. Before I mention the whole question of Christian commitment in the field of politics and social issues, however, I want to mention the matter of "basic communities" or "grass-roots communities" [comunidades de base] and people's varying attitudes towards them.

These "basic communities" are an invention of the Latin American Church. In reality they derive from the Movement for Basic Education (MEB) in Brazil. We have gradually come to discover the importance of a concrete community in which the faith of the Christian finds real affective ties. Such basic communities are now being discussed in Europe, and they may represent a major trend in the pastoral work of the future.

The individual living in urban Christendom is a lonely figure lost in a huge impersonal crowd. When he goes to Church, he often does not know the people on either side of him. There is no intermediary between the concrete individual and the impersonal Church. Something is needed to bridge the gap between the two, and that is what the "basic community" seeks to do. It is a small community in which the participants render each other concrete help and thus empirically experience their fellowship with one another. The impersonal parish community at Sunday Mass is to be transformed into a collection of many such basic communities.

In his small Brazilian diocese of Creteús, Bishop Antonio Fragoso has 150 basic communities in each of his ten parishes. They are the basis upon which parochial and diocesan life is built. Such concrete experiments and experiences are testing grounds for the future. When the proper balance is found, they will be spread to the whole Church. We sometimes feel bewildered by the variety of seemingly atomistic experiments that we hear of, but that is no cause for pessimism. It takes time to develop organisms that will meet the challenge of the historical moment. It is very much a matter of trial and error because there is no ready-made path set out before us.

Some people can only follow a road that has already been paved for them. Other people now realize that following Jesus entails something different. It is a response to one who calls us forth into the desert so that we may build a new future for his poor. That, at least, seems to be the fundamental aspect of the Christian vocation today.

Pastoral activity is not a set of ready-made formulas, telling us how to sing the liturgy or organize a community. It is basically an attitude—an attitude of faith, hope, and charity. If we wish to know how to act pastorally on a given day, we must open our eyes and ears to what is going on around us. It is in the midst of real-life events that we will hear God's summons. Our response to this call may result in a hundred abortive experiments. But one or two may work, providing a model for the immediate future. And the "basic communities" now operating in Latin America seem to offer promise for the future. They may prove to be one of the successful models we are now looking for.

## CHRISTIAN SOCIAL AND POLITICAL COMMITMENT

Many Christians in Latin America switched from being political conservatives to being Christian Democrats. As we mentioned in an earlier chapter, the rise of Christian Democratic Parties was bound up with the overall effort to establish a "new" Christendom. Such parties were professedly "Christian." The problem is that while Christianity can criticize a political system, it can never be identified with any one political system. When it is, we end up with some version of Christendom and all the ambiguity it entails.

A Christian can say that a given political party and its platform is more compatible with the Christian faith than any other concrete party. But he must be ready to change that opinion in a year or two if it no longer accords with the real situation. We must not eternalize temporal realities. There are two aspects involved here: the Christian faith and socio-political interpretation of the real-life situation. Let us see what has gone on in Latin America in certain instances.

The notion of Christian Democratic political parties developed with such figures as Alside De Gasperi in Italy, Konrad Adenauer in West Germany, and Eduardo Frei in Chile. Where Christians were well organized, and where there were strong leftist groups in opposition, Christian Democratic parties have managed to win political power. In other countries, such as Argentina and Colombia, where populist groups tended to be centrist, Christian Democratic parties have never really won power. Today it seems unlikely that such parties will exert the same influence they once did, for many people now feel that they have failed to effect the social revolution they proclaimed. Many Christians are moving towards Marxism as a purely political and economic interpretation of reality. Following the line of thinking espoused by people like Louis Althusser, they feel that they can dissociate Marx's thinking as an economist and social observer from his anthropological and ontological underpinnings. In other words, they feel they can be Marxists in economics and Christians in their faith.

This feeling is open to serious question, I think. If one moves from *Das Kapital* to other writings of Marx—e. g., *Misère de la philosophie, Die deutsche Ideologie,* and the manuscripts of 1844—one finds that a whole anthropology, ontology, and theology underlie his economics. Marx is a panontist, who affirms the totality as divine. This is a fact, it seems to me, and most critiques of Marx are superficial because they fail to take this into account.[11]

The implications of this basic fact are becoming clearer, I think. Some Christians in Chile left the Christian Democratic Party to form MAPU, a Marxist party of Christians. When a Cuban visitor expressed delight at meeting Christian Marxists, the MAPU delegates insisted that in their political gatherings they were Marxists. The Cuban delegate then asked them why they did not join the Communist Party if that were the case. The MAPU members resisted that idea because somehow they also felt that they were Christians. It is the implicit contradiction in all this that has led some to leave MAPU and form MIC, a leftist but non-Marxist Christian political party. Here again, however, they have felt obliged to append the label "Christian" to their political party. To do this is, in my opinion, to use the Church as a tool for one's own political ends.

This is not to suggest that the Christian cannot be involved in efforts to implement socialism in Latin America. The whole question of socialism has been opened up once again by certain Latin American bishops: Cándido Padim, Carlos González, Helder Camara, Sergio Méndez Arceo, and so forth. They have pointed out that there can be a humanistic and Christian version of socialism. The bishops of Peru formulated a strong statement along these lines at their 1971 Synod: "Christians ought to opt for socialism. We do not mean a bureaucratic, totalitarian, or atheistic socialism; we mean a socialism that is both humanistic and Christian." Note that they say "ought to," not "may," opt for socialism; four times in their statement they refer to the "desirability" of such an option today. In his recent letter to Cardinal Roy of Canada, Pope Paul VI noted that certain versions of socialism are incompatible with Christianity. It would seem, then, that some forms of socialism are compatible with Christianity. We have broken through the theoretical knot that once tied up our thinking on this matter.

Back in 1850 "democracy" was a bad word in the Church. Men like Lammenais and Lacordaire were looked upon with disfavor for mentioning such things. Many churchmen came from upper-class families, and talk about democracy and the workingman's rights smacked too much of the French Revolution. Today we are far beyond that controversy, so much so that talk about Christian Democracy seems to be somewhat behind the times. In some circles the Christian Democrat is viewed as a member of the elite who wants to continue discredited "developmentalist" ideas and policies. We seem to be moving towards more serious consideration of socialism.

Some people, of course, may sharply disagree with what I am saying here. My main point, however, is the same one brought out by the Peruvian bishops: "The mission of the Church is to open people's minds and hearts to a consideration of the most pressing and urgent problems."

## PRIVATE PROPERTY

Let us briefly consider the whole issue of private property as an example of the problems we now confront. You will hear people say that private property is a natural right, hence inviolable. The formulation is not correct, however, and Thomas Aquinas would shudder to hear it. To begin with, there is something that is the common possession of mankind. According to the oldest line of tradition in the Church, which would include the Fathers of the Church and people like Thomas Aquinas, the created universe is the common possession of all. This possession comes first, and Aquinas calls it a natural right. We are the stewards and administrators of the cosmos, possessing it in common. The stewardship is not private or exclusivist.

What are we to say about private possession? Saint Basil said that private property was the result of original sin. If human beings had not committed sin, they would share everything with each other and live in a state of justice—without private property. Basil was a monk, and the monks lived a life in common as opposed to the system of private ownership that prevailed in civilized towns and cities.

According to Thomas Aquinas, private property is a *jus gentium,* not a *natural right.* The notion of the "right of peoples or nations" is discussed by a scholastic professor of Salamanca, the late Santiago Ramírez. He explains that private property is a *secondary* natural right. I have a *natural* right to those means and resources which are necessary if I am to achieve my end or goal. The end of man is happiness, and he has a right to those means which will enable him to attain that end: i. e., to food, clothing, shelter, education, and so forth. But what about those means that are not necessary? What about the second car, the second house, and so forth? I do not have a natural right to those things, because I do not need them to attain my end. This is the clear and unmistakable doctrine of Christian tradition. My power over secondary, non-necessary means is merely a positive right; it is not a natural right.

Consider for a moment the Amerindians living on the Argentinian *pampas* before these areas were incorporated into the present nation. Those Indians lived there by natural right because the land and its basic resources were necessary for them. Then General Roca came along, drove out the Indians with his army, and handed the land over to people living in Buenos Aires. Was his action peaceable and just? Who really had a right to those lands—the native Indians or his soldiers? Doesn't it seem clear that the Indians had a natural right to those lands, whereas the soldiers merely obtained a positive right to them?

When someone says that private property is inalienable, he may well be wrong. Private property held merely by *positive* right is not inalienable. Only what is necessary for man's end is a *natural* right; all else is not. As medieval commentators put it: "In case of necessity, everything is common." And here we might well ask the same question that Thomas Melville asked: "If we are not dealing with a case of necessity in Latin America, where in the world can we talk about cases of necessity at all?"

The point is that we do not have to introduce innovations in doctrine here. We have traditions which go back to the Acts of the Apostles that can be applied to our present situation. In theory, then, there is no reason why we cannot contemplate the implementation of socialism. It may not be the best course. It may prove to be a failure. But speaking theologically, we can say that there is no legitimate objection to it in principle.

Some months ago I stressed this point at a meeting of Latin American bishops, and I stress it here today. I do not think that Marxism should be identified with Latin American socialism. Socialism is very much a possibility for Christians on our continent, but it need not be Marxist.

## NOTES

1. See my article, "The Appointment of Bishops in the First Century of 'Patronage' in Latin America (1504–1620)," in *Concilium,* no. 77 (New York: Herder, 1972), pp. 113–21.

2. See *Témoignage Chrétien,* July 31, 1966; English translation: "A letter to the Peoples of the Third World," in *Between Honesty and Hope* (Maryknoll, N.Y.: Maryknoll Publications, 1970), pp. 3–12.

3. For Paul VI's talks in Latin America see *The Pope Speaks* Magazine (Washington, D.C.), 13:229–60.

4. The documents of the Medellín Conference have been published in an official English edition: *The Church in the Present-Day Transformation of Latin America in the Light of the Council,* edited by Louis Michael Colonnese, Latin American Division of United States Catholic Conference, Washington, D.C. Vol. I, Position Papers; Vol. II, Conclusions. The quote here is from the concluding document on *Justice,* no. 3.

5. *Ibid.,* concluding document on *Peace,* no. 16.

6. Gustavo Gutiérrez, *A Theology of Liberation,* Eng. trans. (New York: Orbis Books, 1973), pp. 21–42.

7. See José de Broucker, *Dom Helder Camara: The Violence of a Peacemaker* (Maryknoll, New York: Orbis Books, 1970), pp. 101–02.

8. See Enrique Dussel, *Historia de la Iglesia en América Latina: Coloniaje y liberación* (1492–1972) (Barcelona: Nova Terra, 1972).

9. See Alain Gheerbrant, *L'Eglise rebelle d'Amérique Latine* (Paris: Seuil, 1969), pp. 237–67.

10. *Sacerdotes para el Tercer Mundo,* 3rd ed. (Buenos Aires: Edic. del Movimiento, 1972); *Nuestra reflexión* (Buenos Aires: Edic. del Movimiento, 1970).

11. See my book, *La dialéctica hegeliana* (Mendoza: Ser y Tiempo, 1972). Another book on this general topic will soon be published: *La dialéctica de Karl Marx;* in it I shall try to explore and prove this thesis. See also Enrique Dussel, "El ateísmo de los profetas y de Marx," in *Segunda semana de teólogos argentinos* (Buenos Aires: Guadalupe, 1972).

# 5

# Theological Reflections
# on Liberation

Hegel, the German philosopher, once said that the reading of the daily newspaper was the prayer of modern man. His observation was a profoundly theological one. If a person opens up his newspaper and comprehends God's revelation in the concrete course of salvation history, then he really is praying; for it is in concrete history that God reveals himself. But the truly important news may not be in the headlines; it may be buried away on the fourth or sixth page of the newspaper. Faith has to discern where the important news, the concrete revelation, truly is.

Today we must develop the habit and attitude of trying to discern the import of daily happenings in the light of faith. We must come to realize that day-to-day history is the *one and only place* where God reveals himself to us. We have been accustomed to interiorize the faith, to think that God reveals himself within the soul of the individual. That viewpoint may well reflect the influence of Neoplatonism on early Christianity. God reveals himself before our eyes—in our neighbor and in history. That is the privileged place of divine revelation, for God reveals himself in our neighbor and in the poor.

THE RISE OF
LATIN AMERICAN THEOLOGY

Today we can indeed talk about a "Latin American" theology, a theology which contemplates our own peculiar reality here. I should like to mention a few factors in the rise of that theology, which did not take place all at once.

CELAM (the Latin American Episcopal Conference) certainly had a great deal to do with it. In the process of coordinating activities in all the countries of Latin America, it brought home to us the fact that we are part of a broad socio-cultural grouping. It thus helped us to look for solutions on the continental level.

The first steps involved sociological descriptions, such as those done by FERES (International Federation for Studies in Religious Sociology). They were under the direction of the Belgian priest, François Houtart. Then came economic studies from the Center for Economic and Social Development in Latin America, and other social studies by ILADES (Instituto Latinoamericano de Doctrina y Estudios Sociales). All these efforts helped to point up our sociological structures and their distinctiveness, but as yet theology had not truly entered the picture.

Thanks to CELAM, various institutes developed: for catechetics (ICLA), pastoral activity (IPLA), and liturgy. To provide information to the participants, these efforts started with certain common guidelines and tried to apply them to the overall Latin American situation. As time went on, something new developed out of this. In the beginning the best theology came from people who had studied in Europe and who more or less reiterated the European thinking of people like Karl Rahner and Yves Congar. It was found, however, that this thinking could not be applied directly to the concrete situation in Latin America. Some sort of a gap existed.

Slowly there dawned the realization that we Latin Americans were the victims of cultural oppression. Our thinking was dependent on, and conditioned by, the thinking of people in a very different cultural situation. We could not in fact simply mimic the thinking of European theologians. We would have to start with our concrete situation in daily life and reflect on it theologically. It was this realization that helped to produce a truly Latin American approach to theology.

In an earlier chapter I mentioned Methol Ferré and his criticism of some of Cardinal Suenens' ideas. Suenens had voiced his own criticism of certain points in the papal encyclical *Humanae vitae.* Ferré criticized Suenens in turn because the Cardinal's ideas represented and defended the viewpoint of the economically affluent and culturally dominant nations. Ferré noted the fact that every theology implies some sort of politics, and that Suenens was, wittingly or unwittingly, defending the politics of the advanced nations. We Latin Americans, however, were much more interested in the universal aspect of the Roman Church than in the dominating viewpoint of certain nations within the Roman Church. Let us explore this whole notion of political conditioning a bit.

## THE INFLUENCE OF POLITICS
## ON THEOLOGY AND LIBERATION

Methol Ferré and Salazar Bondy have helped us to realize that we must do our thinking within a basic context of oppression. Hence we must also ponder this very situation of oppression itself. We are forced to look at the overall situation from the bottom of the heap, as it were, and hence our way of liberating ourselves from the present situation will differ from the approach of people in the dominant countries. The affluent societies have one road to take, we have another road to take. And only people within our concrete situation can truly describe the process involved.

It is precisely at this stage of awareness that a distinctively Latin American theology appeared on the scene. It could not appear before people recognized the socio-political conditioning that weighed down upon the Church and the theologian in Latin America.

Let me give you a concrete example of what I am talking about. Herbert Marcuse lives in an affluent society. When he proposes ways to escape from the knotty problems of society, he does so from within the context of an affluent society. People in his affluent society consume too much and destroy too much of the goods of this world. They need a certain asceticism, and they must balance their excessive pragmatism with the spirit of playfulness. The "hippie" is the typical rebel in the affluent society. Challenging this society, the hippie refuses to bathe or to dress up or to work. And since others eat too much, the hippie gives little or no thought to food. Such a challenge would make little sense in our society. Here we must find ways to make sure that everyone can eat enough to sustain life. In short, our problems are different and therefore we must take different paths towards their solution.

Latin America is the only post-Christendom socio-cultural group among the underdeveloped nations. The other underdeveloped areas are very distinct from us in their culture, so their process of liberation will also differ from ours. Our process of liberation will differ from that which must take place in affluent societies and from that which must take place in other underdeveloped societies. But perhaps all these different processes will converge at some point in the future and help to form a new humanity.

In the meantime the Latin American Church has an important and complex role to play both in the history of the universal Church and in the history of humankind as a whole. We now realize that if we do not ponder the great process of liberation, then our theology will remain floating on thin air and never touch upon serious concrete questions. Our new theology is not wholly new, of course. It is actually a rethinking of all our past theology in terms of an eschatological goal. Just as our past mirrors Hebrew bondage in Egypt, so our future goal is the eschatological kingdom. And our present is the journey through the liberating desert of history. The ongoing life of the Church as a process of liberation is an essential tenet in Christian dogma. It is embodied in the notion of "passover" or "pasch," and the life of the Church is a paschal one.

We must realize that we are involved in a passage through history towards liberation. But we must also remember that concrete liberation in history is not the ultimate, final stage either. We do seek the "new man" in history, but this concrete goal is not to be identified with the kingdom of God. Some day we may have to demythologize the notion of the "new man" too, lest it oppress us and prevent us from continually moving ahead in the process of liberation.

## THEOLOGICAL CATEGORIES

Now I should like to reflect on some dialectical categories that are involved in liberation theology. The term "dialectical" should be emphasized, because it points up a difference with older ways of thinking. Much of Christian scholastic thinking was "substantialist" in nature. In other words, it centered around the notion of "substance," and then talked about it as the substratum of "accidents" which concretized and individualized a given substance. By contrast, "dialectical" thinking focuses on the relationship between two things. The dialectical approach is profoundly Christian. Consider the mystery of the Trinity, for example. We talk about the Father, the Son, and the Holy Spirit. Such terms as "Father" and "Son" would be meaningless without each other. "Son" implies a "Father," and "Father" implies a "child." We cannot ponder the Trinity without using some sort of dialectical thinking.

I should like to stress that the notion of liberation is very concrete. It cannot and should not be used in some abstract sense that deprives it of all meaning. The term "liberation" is a very Christian one, deriving from the Hebrew notion in the Old Testament. God told Moses to "liberate" his people from Egypt. This notion of liberation came down through Christianity to such thinkers as Hegel and Marx, and it was then passed along to many of today's liberation fronts. Christians often translate it into such terms as "salvation" and "redemption," but behind all these notions lies the dialectic of oppression and exodus. If we turn liberation into some abstract sort of salvation, then the term loses all meaning.

If we want to use the term "liberation" in a meaningful way, we must be cognizant of the concrete oppression that weighs down upon us. We must realize that sin and its power is oppressing us and forcing us to live in a situation of injustice. Starting from that awareness, we can begin the process—the *concrete* process—of liberation. It is not some vague, abstract risk we take. It is a very concrete risk, analogous to the risk which Christians took in the Roman empire when they denied the divinity of the emperor. When we take cognizance of the oppression under which we labor and proclaim its existence, we face the risk of torture and even death. We cannot continue to live tranquilly within the established order, for that established order is grounded on sin and unjust domination.

Many people make much of law and order. But one must consider what type of order is involved. If the established order is grounded on domination of other human beings, then it should not be respected. To obey laws that are part of such an order is to commit sin. There are times when the legal order turns into an established immorality, when few legal actions are morally good. Within the context of an unjust totality, illegal actions may be good. They may go beyond the injustice of the established order and contribute to the process of authentic human liberation. Liberative action may be illegal in one sense, just as the Hebrew exodus was illegal in the eyes of the Egyptian pharaoh. In another sense, however, it may be supremely right. It may accord with the justice of a new order that will truly serve the needs of the Other instead of suppressing those needs as the old order does.

## THE DIALECTICAL CATEGORIES OF DOMINATOR AND DOMINATED

In liberation theology, then, the first dialectic is that between the established totality and the Other. Within that basic framework lies the dialectic between the dominator and the dominated, between the oppressor and the oppressed. To truly tackle this dialectic, however, we must comprehend the dialectic in terms of our concrete everyday life. Who is the oppressor and who is the oppressed in my concrete situation? If I am one of the oppressed, how exactly does the established order exercise its domination over me and others?

The word "domination" derives from the Latin word *dominus,* which means "lord" or "master." If someone is master over another human being and treats that other as a slave, it means that he has reified this human being. He has taken a free Other and reduced him to his tool; the Other is merely an instrument which he uses to achieve what he wants. It is this reality which underlies the oppression of the oppressed, and it is the one and only sin. To oppress a free human being is to kill him insofar as he is (or was) free: it is to turn him into a dead, lifeless instrument of one's own plans and designs. "Not to kill" the Other is to allow him to be free. That is precisely what love is—allowing the Other to be free and alive as a human being. And if someone truly loves the Other in this way, then he truly loves God as well.

When the oppressor slays the Other as a free human

being, he stands alone and proclaims his own divinity. He becomes an idolater and an atheist. The overcoming of the oppressor-oppressed dialectic presupposes a conversion in the oppressor. This conversion, however, is qualitatively distinct from the process of liberation itself, and the liberation process is the more important element here. When one party rises up and exerts dominion over another person, forcing that other person to accept his totality, it is he who exercises power. In the actual process of exodus and liberation, however, it is the person who is liberating himself that displays more power and vitality. Thanks to the liberative efforts of the person who had been oppressed, the oppressor can then undergo a conversion without being slain in turn.

This means that our people in Latin America must liberate themselves, or else liberation will never come. Women must liberate themselves, or else they will never be liberated. No one enmeshed in sin can do justice. Only the person who is suffering from injustice can do justice. The process of liberation itself is the only thing which will make it possible for the oppressor to undergo a real conversion. Hence only the underdeveloped nations of the world can enable the affluent nations to discover a new, more human model of human life and existence. Our role in the future is an interesting and important one.

## THE DIALECTICAL INTERPLAY OF ELITE AND MASSES

The dialectic between elite and masses is of another sort. In Latin America, for example, we have oppressors and oppressed. But many elite groups are themselves dominated by foreign powers. So the domestic dominator may in turn be dominated by foreign oppressors. In short, there are different grades and stages of oppression in the whole dialectic of elite and masses.

The elite is some small oligarchic group. The masses is the large group which suffers from the domination of some elite. But our domestic elite is in turn dominated by some foreign elite in the United States or Russia. The foreign elite is autocratic, self-appointed, and bureaucratic. There is no one over it, and it is not democratic by any means. This foreign elite dominates our domestic elite, and the latter in turn dominates our people here.

We can describe all this in terms of the Gospel message. At the top we have Pontius Pilate, the oppressor representing the Roman emperor. Below him is Herod, the native ruler and oppressor under Pilate. Then we have the common people, of which Jesus was one. Our Creed tells us that Jesus "suffered under Pontius Pilate." We often do not advert to the fact that there is a note of oppression recorded in the Creed itself, but it is there. The reigning elite could not allow the liberation of the people, for that would end their domination. Sin does not permit people to work justice.

There is then a political situation incorporated into the death of Jesus. The relationship existing between human beings is a political one, and the person who fails to understand this will probably end up implementing or supporting the worst kind of politics—the politics imposed on people by the established order. We cannot simply say that we love our country. We must be dedicated to making our country one which works justice.

What is the function of the elite and of the masses in the process of liberation? Is all the rightness and wisdom to be found in the latter group? Some people think so, naively believing that the masses have the whole solution to any given problem. But if a given people is alienated for the most part, then the role of the masses may be a very dubious and equivocal one. Remember that the Hebrews fleeing from Egypt in the Sinai desert kept complaining about their lot. They kept telling Moses that they had been better off in

Egypt. Moses had to *fight against his own people,* because they did not want to continue in the demanding process of liberation. The point is that the masses of the people, weighed down by a long tradition of oppressive pedagogy, may not possess an authentic yearning for liberation—at least one that is explicit and clearly defined.

In the process of liberation there must be another elite, standing outside the process in a sense and teaching people what liberation truly is. This is the group that will practice what Paulo Freire calls the "pedagogy of liberation." This group will probably always be a minority. It will be embodied in such as Jesus, Moses, the prophets, the Church. The people in this group know that they must get out of the existing totality. They criticize the oppressing party and help to lead the oppressed towards authentic liberation. Hence they are distinct from both groups in some respects.

These basic categories help us to get beyond the simplistic dialectic of elite versus masses, wherein the latter group is all good. An elite is needed to look at the situation critically and see the proper role of the people in the process of liberation. Knowing this, it must then summon the people, the masses, to undertake the task. Instead of engaging in demagoguery, it must stand outside the masses to some extent and engage in liberative criticism of both the oppressor and the oppressed.

THE TEMPORAL DIALECTIC

Another dialectic involved here is the temporal dialectic, the dialectic interplay of past, present, and future. Some people, living in the present, think that the past was much better. In their homes they practically enshrine their memories of the good old days, and they try at all costs to conserve and even mimic the past. They believe in "pure tradition," which in fact is not living tradition at all but rather "traditionalism." Religious doctrine, for example, is something from the past that must be preserved wholly and integrally. Hans Urs von Balthasar has referred to such people as "integralists": i.e., people who want to hold on to past tradition in its entirety, just as it has come down to them. Such people tend to move towards the right and towards some abstract past.

Another group looks towards an equally abstract future. They deny and reject the past, feeling that history will really begin after the revolution. Like the rebellious adolescent, they wash their hands of their forefathers' misdeeds. They look forward to an impracticable and impossible utopia. Such is the attitude of many revolutionary leftists.

In Latin America we also find another strain: the progressivism of the liberal positivist. Many Christians must be included here, for they think that Christianity can carry out its mission while still remaining a component of the dominant elite. These people think they can be two-headed: Marxists in some respects, Christians in other respects; or bourgeois liberals in some respects, Christians in other respects. Both try to blot out any memory of the colonial past, and they rush headlong towards some totally abstract future.

Finally, I would include here the stance of those who take a populist view of the extreme sort. They live in an abstract present, accepting everything that happens without entertaining any plans or principles. Refusing to explore the present in the context of our past, they accept anything spectacular that happens; but they do so in a very superficial way. They thus fall prey to opportunism, and fail to advance a truly revolutionary program. The people, they say, possess the solution to every question. They feel no need to exercise liberative critical judgment on day-to-day events, and so they are swept along by the tide of events.

I think that a truly realistic position must come from an integrated view of our history as a whole. We must be willing and able to shoulder the burden of our real past, so that we can form a meaningful view of the present and formulate a meaningful plan for the future. It would not be simply a centrist position. It would be the pointed thrust of a prophetic vanguard.

Such a prophetic stance is the true one for Christian faith. The Christian prophet operates out of the authentic past of the Church, not to imitate that past but to open up wholly to the possibilities of the future. Merely static imitation of the past is heresy. If one simply repeats the past today, then he is not even repeating the same thing; for the world has changed and repetition of the "same" message means that one is actually propounding a "different" message today. The only way to proclaim the same message today is to enunciate it in a new way, for all the mutable elements of it have changed in the course of history; i.e., the addressee, the idiom, the import. Authentic tradition keeps opening up to an ever new world, proclaiming the ever new message of God to that world. God keeps on revealing himself, explicitating what had been only implicit. Everything has been revealed and realized in Christ, to be sure, but in history we keep on growing and maturing in our understanding of that revelation as we move towards the parousia.

The mere repetition of a past formula is a lie. The only way to speak God's eternal truth is to reiterate it in fresh terms for every new age and generation. God's eternal truth has no past or present or future, but man's history does. In every age God reveals himself to the Church, and the Christians of that age must proclaim what God has revealed to them. If I am living here in Latin America in the twentieth century, then I must interpret and proclaim God's revelation from the historical context in which I live.

The person who merely apes the past is dead. He is entangled in a petrified traditionalism rather than immersed in the vital flow of tradition. Only the person who is truly alive can hear God's summons amid the concrete flow of daily history. People entangled in dead traditionalism have always misinterpreted the prophets. They have never understood Jesus' remark: "Let the dead bury their dead. Come, follow me." To truly follow Jesus is to set out on the uncharted pathways of history. Life must keep opening up to the new and unexpected. Life is creativity and risk, moving into an uncertain future with all the enthusiasm of committed liberty. Life is journeying towards the cross on Golgotha, not staying behind in Jerusalem to commemorate the great events of the past. Life is passing critical judgment on events and the dominating influence of sin, and hence it cannot help but arouse the resentment of those who are wedded to the existing order of injustice.

The Church must be a prophetic community forging a critical, liberative ecclesiology. It must allow people to rethink every stage of its past history, as well as every stage of human history. Thus the economic situation and past history of the underdeveloped nations cannot be regarded as meaningless events in profane history. They must be seen as the result of human sinfulness. Theology has a role to play, therefore, because it can point out the sinfulness in political, economic, educational, and cultural structures.

## CULTURAL DEPENDENCE
## AND LATIN AMERICAN THEOLOGY

Frantz Fanon's book, *The Wretched of the Earth,* contains a foreword written by Jean Paul Sartre. In this foreword Sartre comments on the cultural subjugation of scholars and intellectuals who are born in underdeveloped countries and then educated in Europe. His whole foreword is a moving statement, describing how people from the Third World are taught to parrot the so-called "ideals" of Christian Europe. Since Europeans think that their ideals and ways are the best, they leave no room for native thinking in the countries which are culturally and economically dependent on them.

We are beginning to leave that stage here in Latin

America. Our theology is now cognizant of its own original-
ity and of our own distinctive past. Our theology has a
mission: to engage in liberative criticism. To do this, it must
go back over the past and discover it again—with new,
critical eyes. All this will be fleshed out in praxis, in concrete
action which forwards the cause of liberation.

Some people must start the ball rolling by taking personal
risks. They are the prophets who point the way to the
future. Some unruly young nun, for example, may suddenly ask her community to consider a new course of action. She will be told that it has not been done before. Her
proposal may greatly upset the community, but it may also
contribute to the liberation of her sisters. Unfortunately, it
often happens that such an unruly person is expelled from
the community, even as the prophets of old were shunted
aside and even killed by their people.

We must give thought to concrete praxis, for only such
praxis can pave the way for authentic theology and for the
possible development of a new *Summa*. Such a *Summa* may
appear in the future, but it is also possible that systematic
*Summas* are now a thing of the past. We have to keep the
door open to all the unexpected events that will take place
in the future, waiting for the parousia of Jesus in the poor.

Pristine Judaeo-Christian thought was critical and negative, in the sense that it stood in opposition to the sinfulness
of the established order and left the door open to the
future. In the future our own theology may have to be more
like that: opposed to sinful structures and open to the
Other, wherever that may lead it.

## THE FUNDAMENTAL CATEGORIES

The fundamental categories are "totality" and "the Other."
The structured totality may also be considered the "inside,"
whereas the Other would be the "outside." The "outside"
is the Other in face-to-face encounter. It is in the

acceptance and interplay of "inside" and "outside" that we must live out our Christian mission.

Let me give some examples of this. A local parish would be the "inside," while the surrounding neighborhood would be the "outside." The community of clergy in a diocese would be the "inside," while the diocesan community of Christians would be the "outside." Our traditional, substantialistic definitions of the Church describe it as a "perfect" society. A perfect society is self-sufficient; it has an "inside" but no "outside" to it. In calling the Church a perfect society, we are erroneously anticipating the perfected kingdom of heaven.

The truth is very different. An essential notion in Judaeo-Christian theology is that every totality, every "inside," also has an "outside." Outside the Christian stands the non-Christian. Outside the Church stands the world in which it carries out its mission. And it does not carry out this mission *after* having attained inner perfection. The very nature of the Church is that it is an "inside" open to the "outside." The Church is a totality (institution) directed towards the Other (through prophecy). This is the basic criterion we must use in evaluating every organism in the Church. If we want to determine whether an ecclesial organism is functioning properly, we must ask ourselves how it is operating with respect to its "outside."

A good bishop, for example, may have real problems. But if he is willing to maintain dialogue with his "outside," he will probably be able to work out a solution that accords with the demands of love. As a historian I would say that most outright breaks between a bishop and his clergy indicate an absence of dialogical openness. If a clerical community or a religious order is not truly open to the world, then any attempts at renewal will end up in self-serving egotism and fail to advance their ecclesial mission. If a parish community of lay people rests content in the shell of its own inner life, without opening up to the larger community around it, then it has lost all sense of the prophetic mission of Christianity. The very word "catholic" is a denial and rejection of all sectarianism. If some parish group concentrates wholly on the "saints" inside its confines, nourishing visions of its own heaven here on earth, then it is lost in hellish egotism.

The "outside," the Other, is of the eschatological essence of the Church. If we feel that we are already in the kingdom of heaven, then there will be no prophetic mission and no Church militant. If the parousia has already arrived for us, then there is no "outside" and no reason for prophecy. In truth, however, we live within ongoing history. The kingdom has begun, but it has not yet reached its consummation. The Church has a critical, liberative mission which is to destroy every self-enclosed totality—thereby opening it up to new possibilities of political, cultural, and religious organization.

The role of the Church is akin to that of Moses when he was confronted with the golden calf. The golden calf was an idol, the totalization of something relative into an Absolute. Like Moses, the Church is obliged to destroy such totalizations, moving mankind on towards the fullness of history. That is why the Church does have a very essential role to play in human history.

The Church benefits the people and entities it criticizes by making them more truly human. It thus gives them more real power by liberating them from their oppressive tendencies. If they use this power to dominate people rather than to serve them, then they commit sin. The Church must come along and criticize them again. We Christians, in a sense, are meant to be the locomotive of history. We are supposed to keep moving it ahead towards its final destination and consummation.

This basic attitude radically alters our human criteria. It is not a matter of first organizing our "inside" community completely and then going to the world "outside." We must be open to the Other outside from the very start. Instead of worrying about my own personal perfection, I must open myself totally and frankly to the Other. Instead of repeatedly examining my conscience in a self-centered way, I must follow Jesus to the cross. As he said: "Whoever would preserve his life will lose it, but whoever loses his life for my sake and the Gospel's will preserve it" (Mark 8:35).

To truly carry out our mission, we must ask ourselves how we are serving our neighbors. If we worry about this task and let God take care of our own perfection, we shall advance in perfection even though we do not realize it. This is the heart of the "spiritual life," or rather, of the "Christian life," for man is not Spirit; rather, he shares in God's own Spirit. We are anointed by the Spirit to live the Christian life, to give ourselves generously to the Other as Other.

# 6

# Concrete Pastoral Applications

As we noted at the start, theology is a *logos* dealing with God's revelation in history. And since there is only one theology in the final analysis, this *logos* about God is also pastoral in nature from the very start. Everything I have said so far is also pastoral in one way or another, because speculative theology cannot really be separated from praxis. Theology must interpret God's revelation in day-to-day history. When it is separated from that history and turned into a distinct theoretical discipline, as happened in the past history of the Church, theology will inevitably become decadent.

Right now, however, I should like to deal with a few specific features that must be taken into account in our pastoral praxis. Pastoral activity cannot be guided by recipes. Instead it must approach the ever-changing face of reality with certain basic attitudes and realizations.

## CRITICAL QUESTIONING AND OPENNESS TO THE UNEXPECTED

Whether we advert to the fact or not, we usually approach life and reality with certain attitudes that are almost second nature to us. The traditional virtues and vices are really another way of describing certain attitudes towards

157

people, things, and life in general. The person who posses-
ses the virtue of justice, for example, is someone who loves
the Other *qua* Other; who does not use the Other as a tool of
his own self-interest but rather gives the Other what is due
to him.

It is important for us to have a proper and truly pastoral
attitude. In today's world this means that we must be open
to the novel aspects of reality and be prepared to work out
novel solutions for new problems that arise unexpectedly.
There is no ready-made solution which can be applied
unthinkingly to any given problem. We cannot simply ape
the past, because we are in a period of profound and
thoroughgoing change. We must keep our eyes and ears
open to catch the novel accents of present-day reality. We
must be prepared to look at reality respectfully and attentively if we truly want to render creative, responsible service. In a real sense, we must be prepared to create new
solutions out of nothing. I say "out of nothing" because real
liberty refuses to be fettered to anything. It is prepared to
create new things. There is a whole "anthropology of creation" that is yet to be explored.

First of all, we must realize that we are influenced and
conditioned to some extent by the totality of the world in
which we live. Many judgments and pre-judgments weigh
down upon us. We are part of some group, we are not the
whole of humanity. We are members of a certain class, part
of the Church; there are others besides us. We see things
from a certain specific perspective. If we do not realize and
accept this fact, we will never accept and appreciate our own
finiteness.

Accepting my own finiteness also entails accepting the
fact that the "Other" sees something different from what I
see; or sees the same thing in a different light. Hence I must
be willing to listen to what the other person says to me. I
must realize that I am not God, that I am conditioned by

certain things, whereas God is not. And these conditioning factors estrange and alienate me from other people to some extent.

Suppose I am talking to someone from the working class. My academic background and university training will weigh down upon me to some extent. I will use certain words and certain lines of thought that may not be familiar to that person, whereas his or her viewpoint may seem a bit odd to me. I may be inclined to look down on that person as an illiterate. But the simple fact is that our real-life experiences are different, hence we may not be able to get to the vital core of each other's thoughts and feelings. Anxious as we may be for dialogue with each other, we may end up talking to each other like two deaf mutes. To break the bondage of oppression and domination, we must learn to listen to each other. We must be open to the Other outside us.

## CULTURAL CONDITIONING

Our educational and cultural training may impede communication with other people. To truly realize this fact is to discover that we are not God. It is easier said than done. I live in this particular world, the Other lives in that particular world. Both are real, and we must bridge the gap between them if we wish to dialogue with each other. Otherwise he will not understand what I am saying, and I will not comprehend what he is saying.

Not only is it difficult to proclaim the truth. It is difficult even to point out the way to truth. I may say something which is rich in symbolic meaning to me, because of my education and experience. To another person it may be relatively meaningless. "Behold, the lamb of God!" To me this may unfold rich layers of meaning. To another person it may be a pointless remark. The road to pastoral ineffectiveness, like the road to hell, is paved with good intentions. It is not enough to say something. We must say something that is meaningful to other people.

To find out what is meaningful for another person I first of all must realize that my own world is not the whole world, that the other person has a world too. I must be willing to enter into that other world and to listen to that person from there. I must get over the notion that the other person has nothing to say. He has much to say, but his words and his world are different from mine. If I truly listen to his words and live in his world, then I may be able to say something meaningful to him.

## ECONOMIC CONDITIONING

Economic factors also condition us. I may think nothing of eating meat today, whereas a slice of meat might be a real feast for someone else. Some people still do not realize that there is real hunger in Argentina, that people are suffering from malnutrition and an inadequate diet. Our economic situation is part of our social status, and it makes us part of a class. The notion of class was not new with Marx. It goes back to Aristotle and it is evident in the Bible also. People on different social levels live differently, work differently, and possess different cultures to a greater or lesser extent.

Saving money, for example, is a virtue for the middle class. People of this class want to "be in the money." In the eyes of someone like Francis of Assisi, however, saving money would not be virtuous at all. He wanted to be holy, and grace, not saving money, was the means to that end. One man's virtue is another man's vice.

This whole matter of membership in a certain class is a very serious one. I cannot help but think of the plight of many priests and religious in Latin America at the present time. They came from a working-class background, and it was there that their Christian vocation developed. Then they went through a period of training and formation in the seminary or the religious order, finding themselves ushered into a new social and economic milieu in the process. Some of them also went to Europe for further studies. When they returned to work among the laboring class, they found that they no longer spoke the same language or lived in the same mental framework. Today they are unable to relate to their own original background and milieu. How much better it might have been if they had not been torn away from their native milieu in the process of "forming" them.

## POLITICAL CONDITIONING

We must also consider the conditioning influence of political factors, for it is an important one. To be part of a social class is to enjoy the fruits of its culture and the benefits of its power. Let me give a little example of that fact. When a clergyman has to go down to a municipal office for some reason, he is often invited to leave the long line of people waiting for service and to come right to the front. He readily avails himself of the offer, pretending that it is a mark of respect for the Church or God's minister. In reality he is enjoying the privileges of a class that has social power. Such power, insofar as it exerts domination over others, is sin. Clergymen make full use of the political power shared by their class when they jump ahead in line or use their muscle in administrative dealings.

We often fail to realize that we are engaging in politics. We pretend we are not, and criticize those who do so openly. But only those who profess their politicking have truly realized the influence of political conditioning on the lives of all of us. If we do not consciously advert to our political conditioning, our actions will be determined by it

in a less than human way. We will be the unwitting spokes-
men of the politics of the *status quo,* whereas the professedly
political activity of others may actually be evangelical.

## RELIGIOUS CONDITIONING:
## FOLK CATHOLICISM

We are also subject to religious conditioning, and here the
whole matter of folk religiosity is very pertinent. For example, we may have grown up in an atmosphere of folk religiosity, then moved away from it, and now find it impossible to make any valid judgment about it.

The whole matter of folk Catholicism, the Catholicism of
the people at large, is an important issue for pastoral praxis.
We have gone through several stages of thinking on the
whole matter, and they are worth reviewing here. Up to the
1940s and 1950s, the prevailing pastoral outlook in Latin
America was one of proud optimism. Notice was taken of
the fact that more than ninety percent of our people were
baptized in the Church. The people of Latin America were
Catholics, our countries were Catholic countries. Such was
the boast.

The situation changed when some of our theologians
read what Europeans were saying about the missionary
status of their own countries. France is a mission territory,
said Henri Godin, in his startling book, *France, Pays de
Mission.* Then Alberto Hurtado, S.J., questioned how
Catholic Chile really was (*¿Es Chile un país católico?,*
Santiago, 1941). Theologians began to wonder whether
there was any real Christian faith in Latin America. Our
people, it seemed, were imbued with superstitious beliefs
and practices; magic and miracle seemed to be their major
interest. A new hypothesis was fashioned: only a small
group of Latin Americans were conscious Catholics nurtur-
ing real faith. The rest of the people evinced a vague re-

ligiosity compounded of superstition and fragmentary ideas.

Then we moved to a third stage of thinking about the whole matter. Our theologians suddenly realized that we did not have any solid criteria for judging how real or how solid was the faith of simple people. How were we to find out? In the previous stage, sociological surveys had been in vogue. People went around with their questionnaires and asked questions: Do you believe in Jesus Christ? Do you believe in the Trinity? Do you believe in the soul? Are you an atheist? In many instances the respondents may not have understood the questions or even heard such language before. The fact is that the questionnaires were framed in the context of a culture that itself was alienated from the people of Latin America. Thus their responses were misleading to a large extent, because they answered from within the context of their own *different* world. Fortunately, we have lost some of our passion for questionnaires.

If I want to know what average people think, I must de-culturate myself insofar as I am able. I must try to get into their world, so that I can dialogue with them in meaningful terms. I must enter a new novitiate, as it were, so that I can operate with hermeneutic and interpretative criteria that are more real and anthropological. We are just now beginning to do that. We are coming to realize that faith is not necessarily a matter of educated self-awareness. Consider the faith of the martyrs and the great saints, for example. It may not always have been articulate and learned in its expression, but it was deeply and truly lived in practice.

So now we are beginning to give more respectful consideration to the faith of our people. We have dropped the air of triumphalism, to be sure, but we also feel that an undercurrent of real religiosity may underlie seemingly questionable practices. We are beginning to detect in people's lives a real openness to the Infinite and a real sense of individual finiteness. If educated Catholics really want to understand the feelings of the people, they must be willing to admit that their training may have alienated them from their own people to some extent.

In another work of mine, I explored the songs and popular music of the Argentinian people as indications of folk Catholicism.[1] We often tend to think that people are mute, that they do not know how to express what they are. The fact is that they do express their beliefs, but in many different channels which we are not accustomed to taking seriously. We send out our alienated questionnaires, note the lack of response, and come to the conclusion that the respondents have no real religious beliefs. But they express a great deal of their view of life in popular songs, the tango, folk music, and folk wisdom. We must break out of the cultural mold in which we are enclosed by education and training. We must learn to listen so that we can truly dialogue with people in their world.

## LIBERATION AND "TRANQUILLITY OF ORDER"

We have been taught that peace is the "tranquillity of order." It is a classic definition, and it has geared us towards a respect for order. But, as Dom Helder Camara notes, "tranquillity of order" in a pond is complete stagnation. The waters must be stirred up and fed afresh with clear rainwater in order to be of any real use.

We must realize that it is not enough to feel at home in our world. Everything may seem fine to us, but in fact our cultural world may be peaceful because it is quite dead. There may be nothing left to do but bury the corpses. The only thing we can really do as Christians is open up to the Other; a fresh way of Christian living will appear to us in the very process of liberation. This opening to the Other is an essential outlook and attitude. We must take our place with the Other, pay heed to what is happening day by day, and thus participate in the process of liberation.

The process of liberation itself is the only means whereby we can discover in the concrete what factors are alienating us on different levels. Hence we must involve ourselves in that process. But it is easier said than done. Father J.Y. Jolif, a French Dominican, is a great philosopher. He noted once that the death of the philosopher is indifference, and that only when he is truly dead, as Socrates was, is he a great philosopher. Well, Christians are dead when they no longer disturb anyone, when their prophetic voice is stilled. Christians are truly Christian when their prophetic voice is heard; and it can be heard only when they maintain the risky attitude of criticizing any established totality.

We must opt for liberation in the concrete, shouldering the risks entailed. Each individual can discern for himself where his own option lies, if he remains open to the process itself. To avoid the option is to betray our Christian commitment.

## BASIC FEATURES
## OF A CHRISTIAN OPTION

First of all, in my opinion, these concrete options must be made within *the framework of a grass-roots community* which is sincerely and authentically alive. Some sort of basic community, it seems to me, is an absolute necessity. Lay people probably ought to create communities of married couples on the grass-roots level, not to form little cliques for themselves but to serve each other and people around them. Priests and religious probably should form grass-roots communities of their own, suited to their particular nature but grass-roots communities nevertheless. An authentic life style will suggest many revisions in existing rules and regulations, for these rules and regulations often are imprisoning rather than ordering principles.

It is concrete life within such a grass-roots community

that will truly engraft us into the life of the Church. I would say that we cannot really be part of the living Church nowadays without being a member of such a community. If we are not, we are merely impersonal individuals living in a neutral, mechanical community and attending impersonal Church functions.

We will have to learn how to live and act in the context of such basic communities. A period of initiation and apprenticeship will certainly be necessary because our heads are filled with all sorts of ready-made formulas. We must learn how to divest ourselves of such formulas so that we can approach real everyday life with simplicity and openness.

Second, these basic communities and their members must discover *the critical function of faith.* The task of faith in real-life history is to fight against pantheism; to fight against projects which seek to be absolutized and against people who seek to turn themselves into gods: to fight against sin—man's oppression of his fellowman. This criticism is performed chiefly with deeds, not with words. Jesus went out and mingled with publicans and sinners, and he thereby drew criticism from those who believed in their own righteousness. The critical function of faith is exercised in deeds and action even more than in words, and it calls the established order into question at every turn.

If a person commits himself to this critical function, he will soon discover the meaning and import of the Gospel message. Jesus did not die on the cross because he was a masochist or because he was seeking ascetic purification. He died on the cross because the logic of sinful structures, of the totality, required his death. Jesus criticized the hypocrisy of the Pharisees and others, and so he represented a danger to the leaders of Israel and to the Roman empire. Latin America desperately needs this critical function today. If the Church does not exercise this function, it is dead.

Third, we must commit ourselves to *concrete action on*

*behalf of liberation.* There are things to be done. We may have to write an article, or give a speech, or participate in some demonstration. The police may be waiting for us. That is the concrete risk we face, but we must be willing to dirty our hands in the struggle to liberate the oppressed.

Fourth, we must be *cognizant of the inescapably political function of our faith.* Let me cite Socrates as an example here. Socrates was a philosopher, pure and simple. One day he realized that the Assembly was wrongly condemning six admirals who had indeed lost a battle but who had also conducted themselves honorably. So Socrates spoke out against this injustice because he saw the Other as such. Socrates exercised a critical function within Athenian society and found himself at odds with those who ruled the city. They were forced to condemn him to death, and he accepted the legal penalty because he respected the laws of Athens. He took the cup of hemlock. Socrates was killed for much the same reason that Jesus was killed. Socrates could not see the real sense of his death, Jesus could. For faith casts a critical light on the whole human realm. Christian faith is seen as an enemy by the economic tyrant, the political tyrant, the religious tyrant, and the cultural tyrant.

Power used for domination is the very power of Satan and sin. It is the institutionalization of original sin. The prophet must speak out against such power when he proclaims the Gospel message. The Christian faith has a political function even though the Christian may not seem to engage in politics directly.

## NO RECIPES
## OR PREFABRICATED FORMULAS

Pastoral activity in Latin America cannot rely on recipes or prefabricated formulas. We must work out feasible solutions as we go along. This means that we must learn how to interpret real everyday life. Theology, then, has an important role to play. Once upon a time our priests went to

Europe to get doctorates in Canon Law; it was the sure road to the episcopacy. More recently the emphasis has been on the social sciences: sociology, economics, political science. Today we are rediscovering the importance of theology for critical consciousness-raising. Faced with ever new situations, we must learn how to discern and apply the interpretative criteria imbedded in our faith.

The process of evolution has moved gropingly towards higher forms of life over millenia. Even those groping attempts which ended in failure had their role to play in the overall process. The same applies to our situation today. We must try all sorts of things, respecting plurality as we go along. Unity is important of course, but we must not equate unity with stultifying uniformity. Tradition is a living, innovative, creative process. Each person must be allowed to use his background and talents in our quest for solutions.

The proper attitude for today is well exemplified by Méndez Arceo, the Bishop of Cuernavaca (Mexico). His field of study is history, and he wrote his dissertation on the bishops of Latin America. He has told me personally that he has found history to be of much use to him. It has taught him to open his eyes to various possibilities, and to allow for their tentative implementation. If someone proposes a certain project to him, he allows him to go ahead with it even though it may seem to be very much at odds with past practice. For example, he has allowed priests to get their degree in psychoanalysis when it seemed that this would be useful to the community in which they live and work.

We must not forget the case of Galileo Galilei. In 1616 he was informed of this condemnation by the Holy Office: "That the earth moves is philosophically absurd and theologically heretical." This condemnation was obeyed in Rome for more than a century and a half, and it was taught that the earth did not move. The pages of history tell us that such sinfulness has been possible for the Church more than once.

In seventeenth-century Paris, a priest of the Oratory

named Richard Simon wrote a critique of the Old Testament in which he made many scholarly observations.[2] He said that God could not have spoken Hebrew because Hebrew was subsequent to Abraham; that Moses could not have written the Pentateuch because it narrated his death; that certain books of the Bible were not historical, and that there were many different literary genre in the Bible. Bossuet saw to it that all Simon's works were burned in the public square, and the Holy Office put his works on the Index of forbidden books. Bossuet continued to believe that God had created the world 4001 years earlier, even though Simon pointed out that this would make the Egyptian pyramids older than creation.

My point here is that we must take cognizance of our past history. We must be willing to suffer persecution within the Church itself insofar as unity is confused with uniformity and a failure to make the proper distinctions. Bellarmine and Bossuet equated Christianity with Christendom, and thus they were led to condemn men like Galileo and Simon.

We cannot rely on ready-made formulas, and so we must ask God for more faith. Our faith must have a real prophetic element in it if we are to lead ordinary Christian lives, for ordinary Christians are obliged to engage in liberative criticism.

## CONCLUSION

To conclude this discussion, I should like to allude to a Gospel text: "When these things begin to happen, stand erect and hold your heads high, your deliverance is near at hand" (Luke 21:28). The words "stand erect" here are associated with the Hebrew words *talita kumi,* which Jesus used when raising the daughter of Jairus to life again. Thus to "stand erect" is to come back to life again, and that is what we must do today. Weighed down by suffering, oppression, and pessimism, we must come back to life as Christians.

Jesus tells us that our deliverance is at hand. It is, in two senses. Our life is short, and our deliverance from suffering is not far away, especially if we are truly committed to liberation. But it is near at hand in another sense also. The person who commits himself to work for the coming stage of history here and now is also working for the kingdom of God which has already begun here. We cannot fashion the kingdom of God out of thin air. We must fashion it through concrete historical projects. No specific project in history will completely flesh out the kingdom, but that does not mean we can sit back and do nothing. Some people turn a specific project into an absolute, idolizing their own scheme. The communists do that with communism, for example. But others avoid all commitment and wait for the arrival of an ethereal divine kingdom. That, too, is a mistake. We must commit our lives to concrete work in history. We must feed the hungry and give drink to the thirsty. We must work with dedication and enthusiasm, even though we realize that every specific project is relative, for that is the only way to make the kingdom of God manifest.

The mission of the Christian is not performed solely by building churches. It is carried out by participating in real-life history in its many different aspects. The kingdom of God is fashioned through these projects. If they are not carried out, the kingdom will never come. We must get rid of many of the false antinomies that still weigh down upon us.

When Jesus cured the paralyzed and the sick, he told them that their faith had saved them. We, too, must have faith if we are to be saved. We must "stand erect" and "hold our heads high" because our deliverance is at hand.

## NOTES

1. See *El catolicismo popular en Argentina,* no. 5, Historia (Buenos Aires: Bonum, 1971).

2. See my article on this topic in *Concilium,* no. 47 (1969).

# APPENDIX

## *A Latin American People in the United States*

More than 25 percent of the Catholics in the United States are Spanish-speaking. Besides the more than 15 million *chicanos,* or "Mexican Americans," there are other *latinos* from nearly all the Latin American countries, especially Puerto Rico, the Dominican Republic, and Cuba. Demographic projections based on birth rate and immigration indicate that by the year 2000, 50 percent of U.S. Catholics will be of Latin American origin.

Since the Second World War the *chicanos* have become increasingly aware of their situation:

> *I am Joaquín,*
> *lost in a world of confusion,*
> *caught up in the whirl of a*
> *gringo society,*
> *confused by the rules,*
> *scorned by attitudes,*
> *suppressed by manipulation.* [1]

In 1962, the year the Vatican Council opened, César Chávez began his work with the United Farm Workers Organizing Committee (UFWOC) in California. In 1963 Reiess López Tijeirina founded the Alianza Federal de Mercedes in New Mexico. Thus began the confrontation between the chicanos and the established economic power that would lead to police repression, jail, and the assassinations of chicano leaders. In 1965 the *long huelga* took place in California and in the San Joaquín Valley we saw the

171

dramatic 300-mile march from Delano to Sacramento. Elsewhere, Rodolfo "Corky" González organized the Denver Crusade for Justice. In Texas José Angel Gutiérrez and fellow activists established in 1967 La Raza Unida, a political party which mobilized schools, neighborhoods, and universities, and also founded the United Mexican American Students organization (UMAS).

Such activity increased in intensity and scope. The first chicano bishop was named, Patricio Flores, Auxiliary Bishop of San Antonio. (Chicanos, who make up 25 percent of U.S. Catholics, thus had one bishop, while those of Irish extraction, representing 12 percent of U.S. Catholics, have over half the U.S. bishops.)

In 1971 the Mexican American Cultural Center was established in San Antonio; MACC has become a center for the preparation of chicano apostolic workers. Somewhat previous to this, priests and sisters began to unify their pastoral approach through their organizations, "Padres" and "Hermanas."

The chicanos are indeed a Latin American nation which is becoming aware of its mission.

The reflections which follow were written after conversations with chicanos:

## TOWARD A STRATEGY FOR ACTION OF THE LATIN AMERICAN-CHICANO CHRISTIANS IN THE UNITED STATES

### 1. The Latin American-Chicanos are a "people"

A "people" is not simply a class, for it can represent many classes. A "people" is not a nation or State. A "people" is a group of individuals, a human community with the same language, culture, religion, race. The Latin American-Chicano "people," therefore, represents a specific part of a nation, but at the same time it is something eschatological, beyond, the otherness which summons.

### 2. The Latin American-Chicanos
### are a "dependent and oppressed" people

A "dependent" people is one which has no possibility of exercising power over its own destiny. It is a people whose "center" of decision is outside of it, above it. A dependent people is "oppressed" when political, cultural, economic, religious, and human power is exercised *against* it and on behalf of the oppressor. The Latin American-Chicano people is an "internal colony," a repressed community. Its neighborhoods, its organizations, its classes, its people are "second class." They are despised, humiliated, and degraded. The consciousness of the Latin American-Chicano people is the "consciousness of the colonized."

### 3. The Latin American-Chicanos
### are a dependent and oppressed people
### within an "imperial nation"

Latin American-Chicanos live in and are part of the United States, their historical fatherland. The United States is the most powerful nation of the "center," a center which exercises its power over the periphery—Latin America, black Africa, the Arab world, India, Southeast Asia, China. Its enormous military, economic, and political power not only determines its hegemony over the poor nations; it also establishes through an unequal and unjust interchange an international situation which is obviously sinful. The chicano must not fail to keep this fact in mind, for if one accepts the "system" of the United States as given, one becomes an accomplice to the imperialism which is being exercised on the poor of the world.

### 4. The Latin American-Chicanos must become "aware"

Since they were annexed to the U.S., or since they have come here to work, the Latin American-Chicanos have lived ingenuously under a system of dependence and oppression. Being poor, wretched, exploited, and despised has come to be accepted as a *natural fact*. It is time they became aware that their condition is one of antihuman injustice and that they themselves, their children, their people must self-consciously take control of the situation to which they have been assigned within the "system."

### 5. *The Latin American-Chicanos must become aware in order to "liberate themselves"*

Merely becoming aware is not enough. Organized action is necessary on various levels—unions, politics, culture, the Church. The *essential point* is the strategic goal of the action. It cannot be an action which tends merely to *assimilate* the Latin American-Chicanos into the system of U.S. life today. The struggle must not be merely to *integrate oneself*, into that system. Nor is it appropriate even to *participate* in the system. It is necessary to *liberate oneself*. "Liberation" consists in leaving behind an oppressive situation, as the slaves in Egypt did, and moving toward "the Promised Land," that is, a more just fatherland, a more human social order, a reformed nation. It is not a question, then, of *entering into* the system as we find it, but rather of freeing oneself from oppression in order to change the totality of the system.

### 6. *The Latin American-Chicanos must become aware in order to liberate themselves and "to liberate the poor nations of the world"*

Living in the most powerful nation of the world, an imperial nation, the Latin American-Chicanos must not free themselves only so that the domination of their own country over the other nations of the world might become yet more powerful. On the contrary, since they know at first hand what humiliation is, what economic, cultural, political, and religious domination is, they must struggle so that their brothers and sisters to the south, from the Rio Grande to Antarctica, can also "liberate themselves." Otherwise the Latin American-Chicanos soon will be the most dedicated participants in the imperial system; they will have been integrated into that system which exploits the poor *on the outside,* forgetting that only recently they were the poor *on the inside.* If it is not perfectly clear about its strategy, the Latin American-Chicano movement will be simply "integrationist" on the national level, and counterrevolutionary and imperialist on the international level. If this were to be the result of the movement it would perhaps be better if there were no Latin American-Chicano movement in the United States.

### 7. *"Christian" Latin American-Chicanos are part of a people who must become aware*

Christian Latin American-Chicanos make up the majority of their people. Christians have a very special mission within the task of defining the peculiar features of the people—their religion, culture, style, language, race, history, and self-awareness. The essence of Christianity is to announce prophetically the good news of the reality of liberation in Christ, a liberation which is achieved in history, not by killing Abel, but rather, like the Samaritan, by serving the person who has been beaten and robbed along the road. The Latin American-Chicano people is a beaten and robbed people. Love of *neighbor* is service in the concrete. Latin American-Chicano Christians and all Christians everywhere who want to serve with good will must participate in the process of becoming aware; and to this process they should bring the critical attitude of Jesus, the prophet of Galilee.

### 8. *Christian Latin American-Chicanos are part of a dependent and oppressed people who must become aware in order "to liberate themselves"*

The essence of Christianity, as we have said, is to announce liberation, but even beyond this it is to be ready to give one's life for this liberation. Thus Christians must go beyond any task of assimilation, integration, or participation; they must be dedicated to the historical liberation of their people—an economic, cultural, religious, and political liberation—as a sign of the eschatological liberation in the kingdom of heaven. Latin American-Chicanos have no other evangelizing sign to give to their brothers and sisters than commitment to the historical liberation of their people.

*9. Christian Latin American-Chicanos*
*are a dependent and oppressed people*
*within an "imperial nation"*
*who must become aware in order to liberate themselves*
*and "to liberate the poor nations of the world"*

Charity is ecumenical, worldwide. The horizon for love cannot be simply our own people or our own nation; it must be the whole world. Christians could not witness to the kingdom of heaven if they worked only to free their Latin American-Chicano people—and thus reinforced U.S. domination over so many other peoples of the globe.

The faithful Christian follows Christ along a path which is made only in the walking. For the Latin American-Chicanos in the United States this means a strategy for action which inseparably combines the liberation of their people and the building of a new and more just national order on the one hand with the liberation of all the poor and dependent nations and the building of a new and more just international order on the other.

Thus it is not a question of "assimilation" or "integration," but rather of the "liberation" of the Latin American-Chicanos. Thus it is not a question of Christians trying to "assimilate" or "integrate" Latin American-Chicanos into the prevailing national or international system. Rather Christians must "participate" in the movement of Latin American-Chicano liberation as a sign of the eschatological liberation of the coming kingdom of justice. Come Lord Jesus!

*San Antonio, Texas*
*1974*

1. Rodolfo Gonzalez, *I am Joaquín/Yo soy Joaquín* (New York: Bantam, 1972), pp. 6–7. Armando B. Rendon's *Chicano Manifesto: The History and Aspirations of the Second Largest Minority in America* (New York: Macmillan, 1971) represents an important point in the growing awareness of the chicanos.

# CHRONOLOGY
# OF THE LATIN AMERICAN CHURCH

## THE ERA OF COLONIAL CHRISTENDOM
## (16th–18th CENTURIES)

### The First Steps (1493–1519)

| | |
|---|---|
| 1493 | Fr. Boyl, first priest in America |
| 1500 | The Franciscans in the Caribbean |
| 1504 | Manso, Deza, and García Padilla: the first three American bishops |
| 1511 | The first preaching of Montesinos on the island of Hispaniola |
| 1514 | Las Casas protests against the *encomiendas* |

### The Missions to New Spain and Peru (1519–1551)

| | |
|---|---|
| 1519 | Julián Garcés, first Bishop of Mexico |
| 1524 | Arrival of the (Franciscan) "Twelve Apostles" in Mexico |
| 1526 | Arrival of the first Dominicans in Mexico |
| 1538 | Vicente de Valverde, first Bishop of Peru (Cuzco) |
| 1539 | Founding of the University of Santo Domingo and setting up of the first printing press in América (in Mexico) by Bishop Zumárraga |
| 1551 | F. Sardinha, first Bishop of Brazil (Bahía) |

### Organization and Consolidation of the Church (1551–1620)

| | |
|---|---|
| 1551–52 | First Provincial Council of Lima under Loaisa |
| 1555 | First Provincial Council of Mexico under Montufar |
| 1582–83 | Third Council of Lima under St. Toribio de Mogrovejo |
| 1585 | Third Council of Mexico under Moya and Contreras |
| 1609 | Inauguration of the Guanaritic Republic of Paraguay |

179

*The Conflicts between the Church
and Hispanic Civilization (17th century)*

1620       Carranza becomes first Bishop of Buenos Aires
1638       The Jesuits in the Amazon
1692       Ten Reductions established among the Chiquitos Indians in
           Bolivia

*Decadence under the Bourbons (18th century)*

1738       Foundation of the University of Santiago
1759       Expulsion of the Jesuits from Brazil
1767       Expulsion of the Jesuits from Hispano America
1768       Junipero Serra begins his work in California

## THE ERA OF NEO-COLONIALISM (1808–1962)

*The Crisis of the Wars of Independence (1808–1825)*

1808       First phase of the wars: the new governments oppose
           Napoleon and support the Church
1814       The Argentine is the only independent country. Episcopate
           is almost completely disorganized.
1817       Second phase of the wars: the Church as a bloc supports
           movement for emancipation against the Spanish liber-
           als.
1823       Leo XII sends the Muzi Mission to Chile
1824       Encyclical *Etsi iam diu* of Leo XII

*The Crisis Deepens (1825–50)*

1826       Despoliation of the religious orders in Bolivia
1827       Leo XII establishes direct relations with New Granada (Co-
           lombia)
1836       First direct contact between Mexico and Rome
1845       Bishop Valdivieso begins his ecclesiastical rule

*The Church and Liberal Power (1850–1930)*

1849       José Hilario López persecutes the Church, expels the Jesuits
1850       Liberals in power in Brazil
1857       Freedom of worship proclaimed in Mexico
1874       Lemos in Brazil writes his book on Comte
1884       Secular education in the Argentine (Law 1420)
1889       Separation of Church and State in Brazil
1899       First Plenary Council of Latin America in Rome

*The Attempt to Fashion a New Christendom (1930–62)*

1930      Catholic Action created in Argentina

1955      General Conference of the Latin American Episcopate (CELAM) in Rio de Janeiro

## THE CHURCH STARTS A NEW ERA (1962–  )

*Historic Councils*

1962      Start of Vatican II

1968      CELAM Conference in Medellín (Colombia)

1972      CELAM Meeting in Sucre (Bolivia): Basic change of orientation

# BIBLIOGRAPHY

A fuller bibliography can be found in a more recent work by this author. See Enrique Dussel, *Historia de la Iglesia en América Latina, coloniaje y liberación (1492–1973)* (Barcelona: Nova Terra, 1974), pp. 433–59.

## GENERAL

Dindinger, Streit, *Amerikanische Missionsliteratur (1493–1908)* in *Bibliotheca Missionum*, Intern. Inst. für Missionswissenschaftliche Forschung, Aachen, 1924–27, vols. 2–3 (the first volume, Münster 1916, also contains a generous bibliography); *Handbook of Latin American Studies*, Harvard University Press, 1936–48, University of Florida (Gainesville), 1959, vol. 21; *Indice histórico Español*, Univ. of Barcelona, Teide, 1953–   ; Rommerskirchen, Dindinger, Kowalsky, *Bibliografía misionaria*, Unione Missionaria, 1934–48, Pont. Bibliot. Mis. Prop. Fide, Rome, 1949–   .

*Bullarium, diplomatum et privilegiorum Sanct. Roman. Pontif.*, ed. by Fr. Gaude, Rome, vols. 4–7, 1859–82; *Bullarium patronatus Portugalliae regnum . . .*, ed. by Paiva Manso, Olisipone, Typographia Nationale, 1868–79, vol. 2; *Colección de bulas, breves y otros documentos relativos a la iglesia de América y Filipinas,* ed. by Javier Hernaez, A. Vromant, Brussels, 1879, vol. 2; *Colleción de documentos inéditos relativos al descubrimiento . . . de América y Oceanía* (CODOIN-Am), initiated by J. Pacheco, F. de Cardenas, L. Torres, Madrid, 1864–84 (indices in E. Schaeffer, Madrid, 1946–47); *Colección de documentos inéditos para la historia de España,* Viuda de Calero, Madrid, 1842–95 (catalogue by J. Paz, Madrid, 1930–31); *Colección . . . de las antiguas posesiones de ultramar,* second series, Madrid, 1885–1928; *Colección de documentos para la historia de la formación social de Hispano-américa,* ed. by Richard Konetzke, C.S.I.C., Madrid, 1953–62; *Recopilación de Leyes de los reinos de las Indias* (Ybarra, 1791), Cultura Hispánica, Madrid, 1943; *Compendio bulario indico,* ed. by Balthasar de Tobar, C.S.I.C., Seville, 1954.

F. Almeida, *História da Igreja em Portugal,* Coimbra, 1912–22; B. Arens, *Manuel des Missions catholiques,* Louvain, 1925; R. Aubenas, R. Richard,

"L'Eglise et la renaissance," in Fliche, Martin, vol. 15, 1951; A. Ballesteros y Berretta, *Historia de España y su influencia en la historia universal,* Barcelona, 1918–41; Descamps, *Histoire générale comparée des missions,* Paris, 1932; Delacroix, *Histoire universelle des missions catholiques,* Paris, 1956–58, vol. 1-2; García Villoslada, "Los historiadores de las misiones," *El siglo de las misiones,* Bilbao, 1956; *Idem, Historia eclesiástica de España,* Madrid, 1929; H. Hauser, "La préponderance espagnole," *Hist. géner.,* Halphen et Sagnac, Paris, 1948, vol. 9; K.S. Latourette, *A History of the Expansion of Christianity,* vol. 3: *Three Centuries of Advance,* New York, 1939; R. Levene, *Historia de América,* Buenos Aires, 1940; F. Montalban, L. Lopetegui, "Manual de Hist. de las mis.," *El siglo,* Bilbao, 1952; A. Mulders, *Missionsgeschichte,* Regensburg, 1960; T. Ohm, *Wichtige Daten der Missionsgeschichte,* Münster, 1961; *Idem, Machet zu Jüngern alle Völker,* Freiburg, 1962; L. Pastor, *Geschichte der Päpste,* Freiburg, 1899–1933; J. Schmidlin, *Katholische Missionslehre im Grundriss,* Münster, 1923; *Idem, Kath. Missionsgeschichte,* Steyl, 1924; A. Semois, *Introduction à la missiologie* (NZM), Schöneck/Beckenried, 1952; L. Tormo, *Historia religiosa de América,* Madrid, 1962; vol. 1; G. Warneck, *Abriss einer Geschichte der protestantischen Missionen,* Berlin, 1910; B.J. Wenzel, *Portugal und der Heilige Stuhl,* Lisbon, 1958; A. Ybot León, "La Iglesia y los eclesiásticos españoles en la empresa de Indias," Ballesteros y Berretta, *op. cit.,* vol. 16, 1954.

F. Armas Medina, "Iglesia y Estado," *Est. Americ.,* 1950, vol. 2, 197–217; Ayala, "Iglesia y Estado en las leyes de Indias," *Est. Americ.,* 1949, 417 ff., A. Egaña, "La teoría del regio vicariato," *Estud. Deusto* (Bilbao), 1954, vol. 2, 527–79; A.G.G. Pérez, *El patronato en el Virreyno del Perú,* Tournai, 1937; P. de Leturia, *Relaciones entre la Santa Sede e Hispanoamérica,* Soc. Bolivariana, Caracas, 1959, vol. 1; Lopetegui, Zubillaga, *Historia de la Iglesia en América Española,* BAC, Madrid, vol. 1, 1965.

## HISTORY OF THE CHURCH

Lino Canedo, *Los archivos de la historia de América,* Mexico, 1961. The most important archives in Europe are the Archivo General de Indias in Seville; the Archives of Simancas and Escorial, also in Spain; the Secret Vatican Archives, especially those of the Sacred Congregation of Extraordinary Church Affairs, and the Archives of the Spanish Embassy in Rome; the Bibliothèque Nationale in Paris; and the archives of the various religious orders. In America we have the Archivo Capitular in Lima, the Archivo del Arzobispado de México, and the Archivo de la Nación in Buenos Aires. These archives have not yet been systematically used for Church history in Latin America. While some work has been done on the sixteenth century and the era of independence, there has been neglect of the seventeenth and eighteenth centuries as well as of the period from 1820 to 1900.

*Collectio Maxima Conciliorum omnium Hisp. et Novi Orbis*, by Card. J. Sáenz de Aguirre, Rome, 1694, vol. 4; *Concilio Limana, constituciones synodales et alia utilia monumenta* . . . , by Fr. de Montalvo, Hispaliensis, Vannacci, Rome, 1684; *Concilios Limenses*, by R. Vargas Ugarte, Tip. Peruana, Lima, 1951–54; *Concilium Mexicanum III*, by Fr. A. Loranzana, A. de Hogal, México, 1770; *Concilios Prov. primero y segundo, celebrados en la ciudad de México, Ibid.*, 1769; *Constituciones del Primer Sínodo de Quito*, by J.M. Vargas, Quito, 1945; *Bulario de la Iglesia mejicana*, by J. García Gutiérrez, Mexico City, 1951; G. Icazbalceta, *Colección de documentos para la historia de México*, Mexico City, 1858–66, 1886–92; R. Levillier, *Gobernantes del Perú*, Madrid, 1913–26; *Lima Limata, Conciliis* . . . , by Fr. Haroldus, Rome, 1673; E. Lisson Chaves, *La Iglesia de España en Perú*, Seville, 1943–45; Mansi, *Sacrorum Conciliorum nova et ampl. collectio*, Paris, vols. 31B-48 (1902–15); P.B. Gams, *Series Episcoporum*, Graz, 1957; G. Gulik, C. Eubel, Hierarchia Catholica, Regensburg, 1923, vols. 3-4.

F. Armas Medina, *Cristianización del Perú*, Seville, 1953; L. Ayarragaray, *La Iglesia en América y la dominación española*, Buenos Aires, 1930; C. Bayle, *El clero secular y la evangelización de América*, Madrid, 1950; *Idem, La expansión misional de España*, Barcelona, 1936; P. Borges, *Métodos misionales en la cristianización de América*, Madrid, 1960; R. Carbia, *Historia eclesiástica del Río de la Plata (1536–1810)*, Buenos Aires, 1924; M. Cuevas, *Historia de la Iglesia en México*, Mexico City, 1952; Jose Eyzaguirre, *Historia eclesiástica, política y literaria de Chile*, Valparaíso, 1850; R. Gómez Hoyos, *La Iglesia en Colombia*, Bogotá, 1955; J.M. Groot, *Historia eclesiástica y civil de Nueva Granada*, Bogotá, 1869–70; Guerra Sánchez, Pérez Cabrera, *Historia de la nación cubana*, Havana, 1952, Ed. Hist. de la Nación; L. Hanke, *Colonisation et conscience chrétienne au XVIe siècle*, Paris, 1957; R. Levillier, *Organización de la Iglesia y Ordenes* . . . *en el Perú (siglo XVI)*, Madrid, 1919; R. Richard, *Etudes et documents,* Louvain, 1931; *Idem*, "Les origines de l'Eglise sudaméricaine," *Rv. Hist. Miss.* (Paris), 1932, vol. 9, 455 ff; *Idem, La conquête spirituelle du Mexique*, Institut d'Ethnologie, Paris, 1932, vol. 9, 455 ff; *Idem, La conquête spirituelle du Mexique*, Institut d'Ethnologie, Paris, 1933; V. Sierra, *El sentido misional de la conquista de América*, Madrid, 1944; C. Silva Cotapos, *Historia eclesiástica de Chile*, Santiago, 1925; J. Specker, *Die Missionsmethode in Spanisch-Amerika im 16. Jahrhundert* (NZM), Beckenried, 1953; R. Vargas Ugarte, *Historia de la Iglesia en el Perú (1511–68)*, Lima 1953– ; Mary Waters, *A History of the Church in Venezuela*, Univ. of North Carolina, 1933; Zuretti, *Historia eclesiástica Argentina*, Buenos Aires, 1945.

## GENERAL HISTORY

L. Alamán, *Historia de México,* Mexico City, 1942; R. Andrade, *Historia del Ecuador,* Guayaquil, 1937; G. Arboleda, *Historia contemporánea de Colombia,* Bogotá, 1918–32; A. Argüedas, *Historia de Bolivia,* La Paz, 1920–29; J. Armitage, *History of Brazil,* London, 1936; C. Baéz, *Resumen de la historia del Paraguay,* Asunción, 1910; Barros Arana, *Historia general de Chile,* Santiago, 1930; Bannon, Dunne, *Latin America,* Milwaukee, 1947; P. Blanco Acevedo, *Historia del Uruguay,* Montevideo, 1901–13; S. Buarque de Hollanda, *Raizes do Brasil,* Rio de Janeiro, 1948; P. Calmon, *Historia da civilização Brasileira,* São Paulo, 1940; J.P. Calogeras, *A History of Brazil,* Chapel Hill, 1939; L. Chávez Orozco, *Historia de México (1808–1836),* Mexico City, 1946; González Guinán, *Historia contemporánea de Venezuela,* Caracas, 1909–11; H. Howe Bancroft, *History of Mexico,* San Francisco, 1886–88; R. Levene, *Historia de la nación argentina,* Buenos Aires, vols. 5-6, 1939–47; V.F. López, *Historia de la república argentina,* Buenos Aires, 1913; L. Montúfar, *Reseña histórica de Centro América,* Guatemala, 1878–88; F.J. Oliveira Vianna, *Evolucão da povo brasileiro,* Sao Paulo, 1938; M. Pelliza, *Historia Argentina,* Buenos Aires, 1888–89; C. Pereira, *Historia de la América Española,* Madrid, 1920–26; B. Quevedo, *Compendio de la historia,* Quito, 1931; J.F. do Rocha Pombo, *Historia do Brasil,* Rio de Janeiro, 1905; W. Schurz, *Latin America,* New York, 1949; Vicuña Mackenna, *Historia general de la república de Chile,* Santiago, 1866–83; C. Wisse, *Historia del Perú,* Lima, 1925–28; N. Yargas, *Historia del Perú independiente,* Lima, 1903–17; A. Zinny, *Historia de los gobernantes del Paraguay,* Buenos Aires, 1887.

V. Alba, *Le mouvement ouvrier en Amérique Latine,* Paris, 1953; R.J. Alexander, *Communism in Latin America,* New Brunswick, 1957; J.A. Alsina, *La inmigración en el primer siglo de la independencia,* Buenos Aires, 1910; R. Carbia, *Historia de la leyenda negra hispanoamericana,* Madrid, 1944; F. Carrillo, *El nacionalismo de los países latinoamericanos en la postguerra,* Mexico, 1945; R. Cereceda, *Las instituciones políticas en América Latina,* Fribourg-Bogotá, 1961; F. Debuyst, *La población en América Latina: Demografía y evolución,* Fribourg, 1961; *Encyclopédie de l'Amérique Latine,* Paris, 1954; J. González Rubio, *La revolución como fuente de derecho,* Mexico City, 1952; S. de Madariaga, *The Fall of the Spanish American Empire,* New York, 1948; B. Massé, *Dom Pedro II, empereur du Brésil,* Paris, 1889; T. Mende, *L'Amérique Latine entre en scène,* Paris, 1952, F.F. de Oliveira Freire, *Historia constitucional de la Republica dos Estados Unidos do Brasil,* Rio de Janeiro, 1894–95; M. de Oliveira Lima, *The Evolution of Brasil Compared With That of Spanish and Anglo-Saxon America,* Stanford, 1914; A. Posada, *Instituciones políticas de los pueblos hispanoamericanos,*

Madrid, 1900; L. Pasquel, *Las constituciones de América*, Mexico City, 1943; C. Sánchez Viamonte, *Revolución y doctrina "de facto"*, Buenos Aires, 1946; J. Ycaza Tegerino, *Sociología de la política hispanoamericana*, Madrid, 1950.

## THE CHURCH AFTER 1808

H. Accioly, *Os primeros Nuncios do Brasil*, São Paulo, 1948; M. Aguirre Elorriaga, *El Abate de Pradt en la emancipación hispanoamericana*, Rome, 1941; L. Barros Borgoño, *La misión del vicario apostólico don Juan Muzi (1823–1825)*, Santiago, 1883; J. Bécker, *La independencia de América: Su reconocimiento por España*, Madrid, 1922; S. Bolívar, *Obras Completas*, ed. Lecuna, Havana, 1950; J. Bravo Ugarte, "El clero y la independencia: Factores económicos e ideológicos," *Abside* (Mexico City), 1951, vol. 15, 199-202; P. Calmon, *Espirito da sociedade colonial*, São Paulo, 1935; R. Carbia, *La revolución de Mayo y la Iglesia*, Buenos Aires, 1945; W.J. Coleman, *La restauración del episcopado chileno en 1828, según fuentes vaticanas*, Santiago, 1954; J. Díaz González, *El juramento de Simón Bolívar sobre el Monte Sacro*, Rome, 1955; G. Furlong, *La revolución de Mayo: los sucesos, los hombres, las ideas*, Buenos Aires, 1960; Idem, *El general José de San Martín ¿Masón, católico, deísta?* Buenos Aires, 1950; R. Gómez Hoyos, *Las leyes de Indias y el Derecho Eclesiástico, en América Española e Islas Filipinas* (Univ. Cat. Boliv.), Medellín, 1945; P. de Leturia, *Relaciones entre la Santa Sede e Hispanoamérica: Epoca de Bolívar (1800–35)*, Caracas, vol. 2, 1959; R. Levene, *Ensayo histórico sobre la revolución de Mayo y Mariano Moreno*, Buenos Aires, 1920; L. Medina Asencio, *La Santa Sede y la emancipación mexicana*, Guadalajara, 1946; B. Mitre, *Historia de Belgrano y la independencia argentina*, Buenos Aires, 1902; Idem, *Historia de San Martín*, Buenos Aires, 1887–1888; J.M.L. Mora, *El clero, el Estado y la economía nacional*, Mexico City, 1950; M. de Oliveira Lima, *O movimento da independencia (1821–22)*, São Paulo, 1922; J.B. Otero, *Historia del Libertador*, Buenos Aires, 1932; J. Ots Capdequí, *El estado español en la Indias*, Mexico City, 1941; Pereira da Silva, *Historia da fundação do imperio Brasileiro*, Río de Janeiro, 1864–68; A. Pérez Goyena, "La masonería en España durante la guerra de la independencia," *Razón y Fé*, 1958, vol. 22, 414-28; A. Piaggio, *La influencia del clero en la independencia argentina*, Buenos Aires, 1912; M. Picón Salas, "Miranda: el primer criollo de dimensión histórica mundial", *Rev. Nac. de Cultura* (Caracas), 1950, 78-79, 174-82; P. Rada y Gamio, *El arzobispo Goyeneche y apuntes para la historia del Perú*, Rome, 1917; M. Serrano Sanz, *Orígenes de la dominación española en América*, Madrid, 1918; E. Shiels, "Church and State in the First Decade of Mexican Independence," *Catholic Hist. Rev.*, 1942, vol. 28, 206-28; A. Tormo, *op. cit.*, vol. 3, 1962; A. Undurraga Huidobro, *Don Manuel*

*Vicuña Larraín,* Santiago, 1887; R. Vargas Ugarte, *El episcopado en los tiempos de la emancipación sudamericana (1809–1830)* (Amorrortu), Buenos Aires, 1932; C.K. Webster, *Britain and the Independence of Latin America,* New York, 1938.

J. Alvarez Mejía, "La Iglesia en el Uruguay," *Latinoamérica,* Mexico City, 1950, 23:493-99; J. Bañados Espinosa, *Balmaceda, su gobierno y la revolución de 1891,* Paris, 1894; M. Barbosa, *A Igreja no Brasil,* Rio de Janeiro, 1945; A. Bermeo, "Relaciones de la Iglesia y el Estado ecuatoriano," *Boletín del cent. de Invest. históricas* (Guayaquil), 1947, 298-316; J. Casiello, *Iglesia y Estado en Argentina,* Buenos Aires, 1947; J. Chana Cariola, *Situación jurídica de la Iglesia,* Santiago, 1931; M. Cruchaga Tocornal, *De las relaciones de la Iglesia y el Estado en Chile,* Madrid, 1929; M.P. Holloran, *Church and State in Guatemala,* New York, 1949; J. Lloyd Mecham, *Church and State in Latin America,* Chapel Hill, 1934; R. Pattee, *Gabriel García Moreno,* Quito, 1941; J.P. Restrepo, *La Iglesia y el Estado en Colombia,* London, 1881; C.F. Sáez García, *Apuntes para la historia eclesiástica del Perú,* Lima, 1876; J. Tobar Donoso, *La Iglesia ecuatoriana en el siglo XIX,* Quito (Ecuador), 1934–1935; D. Vélez Sarsfield, *Relaciones del Estado con la Iglesia en la antigua América española,* Buenos Aires, 1884; J.A. Verdaguer, *Historia eclesiástica de Cuyo,* Milan, 1931–32.

Of the studies published by FERES in the series entitled *Estudios socioreligiosos latinoamericanos,* the following concern Church structures: I. Alonso, *La iglesia en América latina,* 1964; I. Alonso, E. Amato, *La iglesia en Argentina,* 1964; I. Alonso, G. Garrido, *La iglesia en América central y el Caribe,* 1962; I. Alonso, G. Garrido, J. Dammert-Bellido, J. Tumiri, *La iglesia en Perú y Bolivia,* 1962; I. Alonso, A. Gregorÿ, *La iglesia en Brasil,* 1964; I. Alonso, M. Luzardo, G. Garrido, J. Oriol, *La iglesia en Venezuela y Ecuador,* 1962; I. Alonso, R. Poblete, G. Garrido, *La iglesia en Chile,* 1962; G. Perez, I. Wüst, *La iglesia en Colombia,* 1961; R. Ramos, I. Alonso, D. Garre, *La iglesia en México,* 1963. In the same series, and in the series *Estudios sociológicos latinoamericanos,* see also: G. Perez, *Seminarios y seminaristas;* G. Garrido, *La ayuda sacerdotal a América Latina;* J.M. Estepa, *La liturgia y la catequesis en América Latina;* O. Domínguez, *El campesino chileno y la Acción Católica rural;* C. Torres, B. Corredor, *Las escuelas radiofónicas de Sutatenza (Colombia);* C.P. de Camargo, *Aspectos sociológicos del Espiritismo en São Paulo;* F. Houtart, *América Latina en cambio social;* J.L. de Lannoy, *El comunismo en América Latina.*

Y. Allen, *A Seminary Survey,* New York, 1960; J.M. Caro, *El misterio de la Masonería,* Santiago, 1947; W.J. Coleman, "Latin American Catholicism," *World Horizons Reports* (New York), 1958. J. Frisque, *Bilan du Monde,* Tournai, 1964, vol. 2; F. Houtart, "Les conditions sociales de la pastorale dans les grandes villes de l'Amérique Latine," *Social Compass,* 1957/58, vol. 5, 181-200; A. Hurtado Cruchaga, *Humanismo social,* Santiago, 1946; B. Kloppenburg, "Der brasilianische Spiritismus," *Social Compass,* 1957/58, vol. 5, 237-56; *Idem,* "O Espiritismo no Brasil," *Rev. Ecclesiast. Brasileira* (Petrópolis), 1959, vol. 19, 842-71; M. Matthei, "Neuland der Kirche," *Benediktinische Monatszeitschrift,* 1958, 351-62; *Idem,* "Klosterstädte," *Ibid.,* 1959, 183-98; R. Pattee, *El catolicismo contemporáneo en Hispanoamérica,* Buenos Aires, 1951; "Perspectives de Catholicité," *Cahiers des Auxiliaires* (Brussels), 1958, 17-4; C. Pape, *Katholizismus in Lateinamerika,* Bonn, 1963; *Rythmes du Monde,* 1961, IX-2-3-4; S. Schmidt, "Panorama general de la Iglesia y sus seminarios en América Latina," *Seminarios,* 1959, 10:187-201; J.L. Segundo "L'avenir du Christianisme en Amérique Latine," *Lettre* (Paris), 1963, 54:1-12; Sireau, Zañartu, Cereceda, *Terre d'angoisse et d'espérance: l'Amérique Latine,* Paris, 1959.